The University of Arkansas Razorback Band

THE
University OF Arkansas
RAZORBACK BAND

A History, 1874–2004

BY T. T. TYLER THOMPSON

THE UNIVERSITY OF ARKANSAS PRESS

Fayetteville

2004

08   07   06   05   04   5   4   3   2   1

Designed by Liz Lester

☉ The paper used in this publication meets the minimum requirements
of the American National Standard for Permanence of Paper for
Printed Library Materials Z39.48-1984.

LIBRARY OF CONGRESS CATALOGING-IN-PUBLICATION DATA

Thompson, T. T. Tyler.
The University of Arkansas Razorback Band : a history, 1874-2004 /
by T. T. Tyler Thompson.
p.   cm.
Includes index.
ISBN 1-55728-779-1 (hardback : alk. paper)
1. University of Arkansas, Fayetteville. Razorback Band. I. Title.
ML1311.T46   2004
784.8'3'06076714—dc22
2004006375

*To everyone who has ever
enjoyed being a part of the
University of Arkansas band program*

and

*my parents,
who introduced me to the world of music.*

"They were always there when you needed them the most. Whether it was to add life to the pep rally or rock the rafters of Barnhill, these were the animals to invite.

"The men and women who comprised the Marching, Hog Wild, Jazz and Symphonic Bands deserved much credit for the time and preparation it took to entertain and excite audiences at the University.

"These musical students made you feel welcomed at your first football game and made you reminisce when you walked across the graduation stage. The background music makers of your educational career."

—from the 1988 Razorback Yearbook

"These are the good ole days . . ."

—Carly Simon

CONTENTS

This is not an ordinary work.

A documented history normally deals with a civilization, a period of time, a significant event, a person, or a people. This book contains a bit of all of these. It is the result of many years of diligent and careful research of the University of Arkansas band program from its beginnings as a band of young musicians in the late 1800s to its culmination as a major college organization seen and heard by millions of spectators in the stadiums, arenas, main streets, and concert halls of Arkansas, America, and Europe. In the process of recounting performances and events, it brings to life the multiple functions and people who have been a part of this history for 130 years.

From ancient times, various musical talents have been called upon to entertain, to signify, or to dedicate important events in the lives of others. The Razorback Band and its companion musical organizations certainly have their share of such occasions in their legacy. From its early beginnings of a military organization, the band's responsibilities of entertaining community, students, and faculty soon led to regular appearances at athletic events. The band grew from a minor attraction for a few hundred people gathered at the sidelines to one that had a nationwide television audience in the 1960s and 1970s. The venues it performed in grew from local parade appearances, to gubernatorial and presidential inaugurals, and even to leading the famed St. Patrick's Day Parade in downtown Dublin, Ireland. Formal band concerts became a regular feature of non-athletic events to the delight of patrons with a taste for serious band literature. Such ventures took the various bands across the country including the Atlantic City Bicentennial Celebration as well as to Carnegie Hall in New York City.

The many times and places cited in the book will revive memories in the minds of those who made the music as well as those who heard it, and significantly, recounted the events. That combination of people, places, and occurrences is what this book is all about.

ELDON JANZEN
Director Emeritus
University of Arkansas
Razorback Band
December 2003

I remember the magical moment as if it were yesterday—my first performance as a member of the University of Arkansas Razorback Band in September 1974. It was the first game of a new year, and War Memorial Stadium was packed with its usual rowdy sold-out crowd of Hog fans. As the band entered the stadium to begin the parade around the field and the announcer heralded our entrance, I wondered if goose bumps would literally tear through my uniform. I don't remember how many notes I actually played that night because I was so overwhelmed with the awesome feelings of pride and absolute amazement that I had been given the privilege of being a member of this very special group of people. Little did I know at the time just how many wonderful memories awaited me, not to mention that someday I would get the opportunity to live a dream I had dared to imagine many years earlier as an eighth grader growing up in Hope, Arkansas—to be the director of the Razorback Band and be given the responsibility for the day-to-day operation of the total band program.

Four of the best years of my life were spent as a member of the Razorback Band —from 1974 to 1978. Much of who I am and what success I now enjoy can be credited to the wonderful leadership of Mr. Eldon Janzen, Director of Bands for twenty-five years, and to many of my fellow students who helped me with their wonderful lessons of leadership, often leading more by example than verbally. Being a member of the Razorback Band is often a life-changing experience for the better. The older I get, the more I appreciate all that my membership gave to me. One of my dear friends, Mr. Lewis Epley Jr., constantly reminds us of what being a member of the band did for him at a difficult time in his life. I am sure that there are literally thousands of positive testimonials that could be shared by band alumni if they were only given the opportunity to do so.

Over the past few years, the Razorback Band has grown and continues to expand in many ways—in numbers, quality, and stature. While the band has always received at least a measure of respect across the university landscape, it has recently taken a quantum leap in priority and visibility. There are many people to thank for this, but the number-one reason that we currently enjoy the successes we do is the wonderful work of the students, staff, and directors who have gone before us. The Razorback Band is constantly and consistently recognized in numerous publications across campus and our state. We were selected to be one of the organizations allowed to participate in the university-wide Campaign for the 21st Century with a goal of raising five million dollars in five years. We receive consistently high marks from our fellow institutions for our high level of performance and our hospitality for our visiting bands. Membership in the Razorback Band is truly special!

Today, there are seven bands in the band division. The four athletic bands are the Razorback Marching Band, the Hogwild Basketball Band, the Lady Hogwild Basketball Band, and the Lady Hogwild Volleyball Band. The three concert bands are the Wind Symphony, the Symphonic Band, and the Concert Band. All the ensembles continue to excel and improve each year. The athletic bands continue to get the opportunity each year to represent our university and state at bowl games and tournaments across the region and the country. In 2000, the Wind Symphony, under the direction of W. Dale Warren, had the honor of performing in Carnegie Hall in New York City.

This book truly captures the flavor and essence of the long and rich history of the Razorback Band. Kudos to Dr. Tyler Thompson for his many, many hours of meticulous work in compiling the history of our band from its very beginning, both in text and in pictures. I firmly believe that we would not be enjoying the successes we do in the modern day without the blood, sweat, and tears shed by the thousands of band alumni and the leadership exhibited by our past directors. Through the years, the Razorback Band has played an integral role in the life of the Fayetteville campus, often not getting near the credit it deserves for its accomplishments. I encourage you to start at the beginning of this book and familiarize yourself with the great names of the past who helped build the band program. To be knowledgeable of our history is the point of truly being able to appreciate just how special it is to be a member of the Razorback Band family.

TIMOTHY GUNTER
Director of Athletic Bands
University of Arkansas
December 2003

In the fall of 1967 I entered the University of Arkansas as a freshman after having graduated from Pine Bluff's Dollarway High School in the spring. Having played alto saxophone in the Dollarway Bands from the sixth grade until commencement, I had enjoyed all the activities being a member of the band entailed: playing at football and basketball games, marching in numerous parades, and performing concerts for the local community and at festival contests. I also was fortunate enough to have served my last two years as the band's drum major.

Upon applying to the U of A, I was encouraged to tryout for the Marching Razorback Band. But I decided that for once in my life I wanted to be a "normal" student, one who went to ballgames and cheered in the stands just like the majority of the student body. Being a freshman coming from a small high school and entering the "huge" university, I didn't think I needed the extra distraction of the Razorback Band competing for time necessary for my studies.

So, when I arrived in Fayetteville, I was enrolled with a full slate of sixteen hours and, with the rest of the ten thousand students on campus, began my college career. Here and there I would run into people whom I had met during high school at band camps and various band competitions and ballgames across the state. Many were already members of the Razorback Band and encouraged me to join in the fun. But I held fast and wished them well.

During the second week of classes, a pep rally was held in the Greek Theater for the season's first football game in which Arkansas was to face Oklahoma State in Little Rock, and I went with a bunch of guys on my floor in the dormitory to the event.

In the semicircular Greek Theatre with its majestic columns proudly erect on the side of the hill facing Dickson Street, hundreds of students were packed into the seats according to their respective living groups. Sororities, fraternities and dormitories all displayed banners and standards identifying their importance, and each group proclaimed their superiority over the others. The excitement was deafening and electric, reflecting a kind of school spirit I had never experienced in high school.

But the electricity of the evening would rev up even higher. All of a sudden, at the moment that the pep rally was to start, a muffled drum cadence began somewhere off in the distance. One couldn't see where it was coming from because of the trees and bushes lining the backside of the Greek Theatre. But it was coming from somewhere back there, it was becoming louder with each passing second, and it was getting closer. After a few minutes, the loud drum cadence was accompanied by seemingly hundreds of marching feet and a chant of "Go, Hogs, Go!!" The students in the theater were delirious in their yelling, and it appeared that the whole scene was one of barely controlled mayhem.

The cheerleaders invaded the theater's stage, jumping and tumbling, and everyone exhibited a collective smile of excitement at the beginning of this Hog celebration. Then all of a sudden the drum cadence stopped, and everyone began calling the Hogs. At the end of the cheer, drummers from the band came from both sides of the theater down front and lined up in the grassy area at the bottom of the steps leading all the way to the back of the theater. Then the percussionists started up another cadence, this time a double-timed one which inspired everyone standing on their seats to clap along with them. At the same time, band members two abreast and swinging their instruments from side to side in unison started high-stepping it down the center aisle from top to bottom toward the drummers, veering off to either side at the bottom of the steps and then entering the stage from the arched entrances on the right and left. The band members in their matching pep-rally sweatshirts just kept coming and coming down those steps. It seemed as though there were a thousand of those folks, though the number was more like a hundred and fifty. By the time the whole band was on stage, including majorettes punching the air with their batons to the pulsating beat and featured twirlers juggling multiple airborne missiles, the drum majors gave a whistle for the "Fight Song," and the whole outdoor arena just exploded with Razorback adrenaline.

For the next thirty minutes, it was like being in the middle of a supercharged circus. Each living group whooped and hollered like its very existence depended on it, the cheerleaders incited the crowd with each new cheer like throwing gasoline on a fire, and the emcees worked themselves into a frenzy trying to be funny and enthusiastic. The band looked like the happiest of families enjoying each other as part of those joyous festivities, and I was aching to be a part of it up there on that stage. It was thrilling to be a part of the audience watching the show unfold and reacting to the glorious flash and dash on stage, but somehow I didn't seem to be in the right place. I could be up there doing what they were doing and having the time of my life, couldn't I?

After numerous cheers, introductions, and music, it was time for the pep rally to come to a close. The cheerleaders began one last "Call the Hogs," and the band started to leave the stage. Once again the drum section struck up a snappy cadence, and the band members started high-stepping it off the stage toward the center aisle and up those steps onto the street. Then the drummers proceeded to sail up those steps with the drum majors following. Soon, a couple of whistles were heard, and the band proceeded to march away from the rally with their cadence eventually fading into the distance.

Needless to say, I had been mesmerized by the experience and had been totally impressed by the Razorback Band. The next day I went to the band building and introduced myself to the band director, Dr. Richard Worthington, "Doc" to anyone who ever knew him. I asked him if it were too late to join the band. He told me to come by on Monday, and he'd see if there might be a position into which he could fit me.

And that was it. Come Monday I got his okay and was an official member of the Marching Razorback Band having added the one-hour credit course to my schedule through the registrar's office. And I remained a member of that band for four years serving as a drum major for the last two. So much for being a "normal" University of Arkansas college student.

Being exposed to the spirit of the Marching Razorback Band can be infectious. Just ask anyone who's ever enjoyed serving as one of its members.

Many a college student thinks that the most important time that a college or university ever witnessed was during the days that he or she spent on the campus because, after all, that's when he or she was there. Most alumni can remember fairly accurately the events that occurred on campus while they attended school, or at least what one thinks is accurate (this tends to get challenged somewhat during class reunions, however). But the fact is that other than the time that one personally has spent on a campus, the complete history of a school's story is often murky at best. And the same can be said for the history of the Razorback Band. I can be pretty factual about what I remember during my years with it, but I am pretty fuzzy about the years on either side. Hence, the reason for this book—finding out as much as possible about the existence of the Marching Razorbacks from the earliest mention of a band on the Fayetteville campus in the 1800s all the way to the present.

In the course of researching this book, I encountered many wonderful former band members from the 1930s onward and enjoyed their many anecdotes and tales from days gone by.

Also I have perused *Cardinal* and *Razorback* yearbooks printed for the university, and scanned every issue of the *University Weekly* and the *Arkansas Traveler* that I could get my hands on. And I have the wonderful archives of the Mullins Library and the ever-gracious and helpful librarians on the Fayetteville campus to thank for those resources. Additionally, I found very helpful many articles and photos from state and local Arkansas newspapers even though the quality of the early pictures is not as good as I would have wished. I found the catalogs of the Arkansas Industrial University to contain the most information about the band before the time of student campus publications, along with the catalogs of the University of Arkansas in the early to middle 1900s.

In the stacks of the Mullins Library, I came upon a thesis written by Michael Raymond Considine in partial fulfillment for his master's of history degree in 1986 entitled, "The History of the Military Education at the University of Arkansas." I discovered therein numerous references to the cadet band during the formative years of the university.

A gold mine of information was struck in being able to visit and reminisce with former band directors who still display the feistiness that made them so formidable during their tenures atop the podium. They include my two former band directors Dr. Richard R. "Doc" Worthington and Prof. Eldon Janzen and their successors, Chal Ragsdale, Jim Robken, W. Dale Warren, and the current conductor, Tim Gunter.

Especially rewarding for me were telephone calls and a personal visit I was fortunate enough to have with Ruth Marty and Sybil Cheesman, the widow and daughter respectively of E. J. Marty, the U of A band director from 1948 to 1955. In addition to being thoroughly entertaining hostesses, they helped to add further insight concerning the band's transition from being associated with the ROTC Department to a division of its own within the Music Department.

Very helpful also were the still-keen mind and sharp memory of Roger Widder in his reading over an early draft I wrote. His time spent as the band's transition director between Marty and Worthington provided a valuable vantage point from which to observe the band's progress.

Also, among many others, I had the pleasure of speaking with Lois Colbert, the daughter of Judah Foutz, band director from 1927 to 1940; Earlene Upchurch Little, the first woman documented to have ever served as a regular band member in the fall of 1935; Charles Yarrington, a two-year veteran of the band in the early 1930s; and the late Jimmy Baker, drum major and featured performer of the band in 1939.

Additionally, the scrapbooks which Lambda Chapter of Kappa Kappa Psi and Psi Chapter of Tau Beta Sigma put together over the years and made available to me were most illuminating. Also, most helpful were the video and photo archives of the Razorback Band Alumni Association, which Bill and David Woolly and Don King have maintained for the better part of forty years as a labor of love for the Razorback Band. Further, I am indebted to Jerl Dean and Jim Beaty for the use of their personal photos for the most recent years covered in this book.

Unfortunately, in 1962 a nighttime fire destroyed the existing band building and most of its contents, including many one-of-a-kind photos and documents. But many individuals who were part of the band prior to that time have been most benevolent in sharing personal memorabilia.

No one researching any organization against the backdrop of the University of Arkansas can possibly do so without referencing three general histories for an understanding of the context in which the band developed and matured along with the school's growth. The histories to which I am referring are *History of the University of Arkansas* by John H. Reynolds and David Y. Thomas, 1910; *University of Arkansas 1871–1948* by Harrison Hale, 1948; and *The First 100 Years—Centennial History of the University of Arkansas* by Robert A. Leflar, 1972.

Though the above authors gave little space to the mention of an Arkansas Band within their covers, they did recognize the existence of the organization and offered some clues as to where I might look for more information.

A fourth book, authored by Dr. Ethel C. Simpson and entitled

Image and Reflection is a visual walking tour of the University of Arkansas throughout the years and includes a few valuable snapshots of early band members.

No single book covering a time span of almost 130 years can possibly include everything on a subject. But hopefully this book will cover the moments that are highlights and give credence to its history. That is what I have tried to do regarding the years during which an organized student band has been in existence at the University of Arkansas in Fayetteville.

Numerous mentions are made with regard to the athletic teams at the school (football and basketball in particular) because many of the band's appearances and successes have been and still are tied to sports. But the main emphasis in this book has been to focus on the evolution and development of the band as the University of Arkansas grew.

The reader may notice that I have labeled the latter chapters of this book with the names of the men who have served in the position as director of the Razorback Band. This is not to say that their service to the U of A band program is limited to the time spans included within the chapters. It is simply a convenient technique to divide up the band's story. Even though the chapter entitled "The Marty-Widder Years" ends with the school year 1955–56, Professor Widder continued on the music faculty of the university for many years thereafter. Similarly, Eldon Janzen's chapter concludes in 1985, though he remained as the Director of Bands until 1995 and serves as Director of Bands Emeritus as of this writing.

Finally, I'd like to thank Lawrence Malley for his guidance and patience in getting this book finished, Brian King for his meticulous editing skills in keeping me honest with the story, and Liz Lester (a former Razorback Band member) for her design expertise in making this book presentable. These three members of the University of Arkansas Press kept my spirits high and constantly encouraged me that this book would indeed see the light of day. I will forever be in their debt.

I apologize in advance for any omissions or errors that may have occurred within these pages, but I also am pleased to have had the opportunity to put together this account for you the reader.

T. T. TYLER THOMPSON
(a.k.a. Tommy Thompson)
January 2004

ost University of Arkansas alumni know that the school began as a land-grant university in 1871 as is inscribed in the university's official seal. What most of them do not know is that there was an attempt to create a system of federal land grants for the establishment and maintenance of state universities all across the country as early as 1827. In fact the U. S. Congress allocated two townships of federal land to be set aside in the territory (Arkansas did not become a state until 1836) "for the use and support of a university within said Territory, and for no other use or purpose whatsoever."

The sale of these lands was to provide an account of funds whereby a state university could be started. Constant arguing between federal and state officials on how the act should be implemented slowed progress considerably. Also land prices were depressed in the Arkansas Territory, and even when some of the land was eventually sold, the bank into which the funds were deposited failed. Another problem was that squatters who were on these lands would not leave, and officials wouldn't evict them. Some of the squatters, in time, even received deeds to the land on which they were living. The program failed miserably in Arkansas.

In 1862, Cong. Justin S. Morrill introduced a land-grant bill after having submitted a previous one that died in 1857 because of a veto by then-President Buchanan. But in 1862 the bill, the Morrill Act, passed with the signature of Abraham Lincoln and entitled each state to 30,000 acres of public land per senator and representative it had in Congress. Since Arkansas had two senators and three representatives, 150,000 acres of land were allotted for the state to be able to sell with the proceeds going toward the building of a state university with the following caveat:

> to the endowment, support and maintenance of at least one college where the leading object shall be, without excluding other scientific and classical studies, and including military tactics, to teach such branches of learning as are related to agriculture and mechanic arts, in such manner as the legislatures of the states may respectively prescribe, in order to promote the liberal and practical education of the industrial classes in the several pursuits and professions in life.

The 1862 act required that each state have a land-grant college up and running within five years. But an 1866 amendment allowed the

CHAPTER 1

The Beginnings of a University

"reconstructed" southern states another five years to comply. Therefore, Arkansas had to have a school in place and in operation by February 12, 1872. Though the Arkansas General Assembly accepted the terms of the Morrill Act as early as 1864, it wasn't until the legislative session of 1871 that that body passed a law establishing the Arkansas Industrial University. The lawmakers also appointed a board of trustees to meet in September of that year for the examination of bids from Arkansas communities wanting the new school built in their town. Though a number of towns and counties were interested, only Batesville and Fayetteville came through with bona fide complete proposals. (Prairie Grove and Viney Grove made the effort, but Batesville and Fayetteville were the only ones seriously considered.) After on-site visits, it was decided on November 15 that Fayetteville would be the location for the new land-grant college in Arkansas.

The board of trustees arranged for the purchase of the 160-acre farm home owned by William McIlroy about a mile northwest of town for the new campus. The six-room McIlroy home was hardly large enough for a new school, so another small frame building was quickly erected as an adjunct to the farmhouse in time for classes to begin on January 22, 1872.

Eight students were enrolled at the Arkansas Industrial University on opening day, though all of them had certain educational limitations. Therefore, all of these young people were admitted as preparatory students, and more were enrolled as the semester commenced. It was decided by the faculty henceforth to establish a preparatory school along with the university proper and the normal school (a normal school was for the training of future public-school teachers).

In September of 1872, the first collegiate freshman class consisting of four males and six females enrolled along with ninety-one preparatory students. Added to the faculty that month was Capt. Henry L. Burnell, a former officer in the United States Army, assuming the position of commandant and military science instructor, being replaced in that position in 1873 by Lt. Edwin S. Curtis. A graduate of the United States Military Academy, Curtis brought with him all the training and expectations to educate the young male students to be good soldiers.

All male students enrolled were required to participate in military science courses and were expected to wear their uniforms at all times while on campus (though many of the boys could only afford partial uniforms). Marching drills occurred daily on the lawn, weather permitting, and male students had to march from one class to another, including chapel. Segregation of the classes according to gender was strictly enforced, with girls on one side of the room and boys on the other. In fact, no fraternization was allowed between males and females except on rare social occasions. The atmosphere reflected, in all regards, that of a military school, except for the fact that females were allowed to attend classes with the men.

A "commencement" program was held after each spring semester beginning in 1872, though there were no graduation ceremonies until 1876 when nine graduates received their diplomas, including three of the preparatory students who had been among the original enrollees in January 1872. A series of articles printed in the spring and summer of 1874 in the *Fayetteville Democrat* chronicled how university president A. W. Bishop and music professor W. D. C. Botefuhr led a fundraising campaign to purchase instruments for a band to be established on the campus. They accomplished this by holding a number of concerts in the University Hall (later nicknamed Old Main) auditorium, including a variety of vocal, instrumental, and dramatic performances and charging from twenty-five cents to fifty cents for admission. The second annual report of the AIU presented to the board of trustees published in August 1874 makes a mention that "a brass band of fourteen pieces, organized for special use, in connection with the Military Department of the University, and composed entirely of students, has already demonstrated its usefulness."

Based on the evidence of the above, it appears that the birth of the University Band in Fayetteville occurred sometime during the spring of 1874. And on the following pages the reader will find that there has been a band on campus each succeeding year down to the present.

Fayetteville Democrat - March 21, 1874

A University Band.

We learn from President Bishop that instruments of the most approved style and construction for a brass band have been ordered for the Arkansas Industrial University. The students are eager to have them, and the band, thoroughly organized and carefully trained, as is intended shall be the case, will be of great service, especially to the Military department of the University. The town also has an interest in the matter, for this band will be one of its permanent institutions, and while President Bishop has assumed the responsibility of ordering instruments, their expense is greater than, at present, the University can bear alone, and it has therefore been proposed that a series of Concerts be given to aid in defraying the expenditure. These Concerts will be in charge of Prof. Botefuhr, and the first will be given at the Court House on the 2nd of April. Tickets will be sold in advance, and next week we will publish the programme. Three or four Concerts in all, will probably be given, with intervals of three or four weeks between them. The interest taken is, from what we can learn very encouraging, and we do not doubt but that on every night the Hall will be filled. The price of tickets will be fifty cents.

Fayetteville Democrat - April 4, 1874

The Concert

On Thursday evening for the benefit of the University Band, was a success. A large and appreciative audience were present, most of whom we believe were highly pleased at the entertainment. The exercises were of the highest order, and reflects great credit upon Prof. W. D. C. Botefuhr, teacher of music in the University, who was in charge of the concert. We cannot particularize when all did so well. We hope soon to enjoy another of these splendid entertainments.

These three articles are the first mention of a cadet band on the AIU campus in 1874 with the Second Report of the AIU of 1874 corroborating the band's existence.

JULY 11, 1874
FAYETTEVILLE DEMOCRAT WEEKLY

The Inauguration.

Friday last the exercises of commencement week at the University, closed with the inauguration of Gen. Bishop, the President elect. Some changes in the programme of exercises as heretofore announced, having become necessary by reason of the creation of a new Board of Trustees, it was further determined to have different exercises as originally contemplated, consolidated into one occasion. The ceremonies, therefore took place at night on the University grounds. A very large stage was erected, the grounds were lit up with lanterns, and in the end this action of the committee of arrangements in determining to have the inauguration out of doors, was fully justified by the very large audience present, which it would have been utterly impossible to have accommodated either in the hall of the University or at the Court House.

At half past 6, the people were called to order by Dr. P. M. Cox, the President of the day, and the exercises were opened by prayer from Rev. S. K. Hallam.

The address in behalf of the town of Fayetteville was to have been delivered by Hon. Lafayette Gregg, but owing to sudden illness he was unable to be present and a letter from him handsomely referring to what Fayetteville had done for the University was read by Prof. Leverett. Next in order came music by the University Band and then a number of addresses with music from the Euterpean and Philharmonic societies interspersed.

President Bishop received his honors with becoming modesty, fully realizing the high responsibility of the office to which he has been chosen. His inaugural address was an eloquent, dignified, and scholarly effort. Gen. Bishop is alive to the subject of education, full of energy, and will fill the office of President of the Arkansas Industrial University with credit.

The exercises closed with a benediction from Rev. T. B. Ford.

SECOND REPORT

OF THE

Arkansas Industrial University,

WITH A

NORMAL DEPARTMENT THEREIN.

LOCATED AT

FAYETTEVILLE, WASHINGTON COUNTY, ARK.

ORGANIZED SEPTEMBER 18, 1871.

AUGUST, 1874.

LITTLE ROCK:
PRINTED AT THE GAZETTE BOOK AND JOB PRINTING OFFICE.
1874.

BAND.

A brass band of fourteen pieces, organized for special use, in connection with the Military Department of the University, and composed entirely of students, has already demonstrated its usefulness.

The construction of University Hall, Old Main, was begun in 1873 and completed in 1875. Like the rest of the faculty, Lt. Edwin S. Curtis welcomed the move to a better facility. But unfortunately his armory was assigned to the damp north wing of the basement. His office was located in room number 4 on the first floor immediately south of the east entrance, and the front lawn served as a drill area for more than one hundred years.

Though Curtis had the support of university president A. W. Bishop in his military training, the resignation of President Bishop in 1875 led to the eventual disagreement with his interim successor, President Noah P. Gates. Lieutenant Curtis resigned his position in 1876. Gates appealed to the U. S. War Department to send a replacement for Curtis, but they indicated that no one was available at the time, and none would be forthcoming for the next twelve years.

In June of 1877, retired Confederate general Daniel Harvey Hill was hired as the new president of the university. Hill subsequently enlisted former Confederate colonel Oliver C. Gray as the new professor of mathematics and civil engineering, with the additional responsibilities of heading the Military Department as its commandant. Gray set up the cadet battalion "consisting of the entire body of male students," organized into a headquarters staff, three line companies, and a twelve-member cornet band.

The "Annual Report of the Arkansas Industrial University" for each year from 1874 to 1879 makes a mention similar to the one made in 1874 about there being a cadet band in existence on campus in connection with the Military Department. There is no indication that a faculty officer was in charge of the music and marching direction. It is presumed that an upperclassman took on the responsibility for rehearsing and leading this small group of men.

In 1880 the "Annual Report" listed twelve members of the AIU Band by name among the roster of Battalion AIU Cadets. Included were W. E. Massie as first leader and instructor and F. T. Daugherty as second leader.

It must be remembered that the primary mode of transportation at the time of the early 1870s was by horse and wagon with the occasional stagecoach. The railroad was beginning to expand to the more rural areas, but by the mid-1870s, a rail line extended only as far west from Little Rock as Clarksville. From Clarksville, one had to take a

CHAPTER 2

A Band on the Campus

1874–1908

stagecoach to Fort Smith and then to Fayetteville; this could take days on the primitive roads in the area.

By 1878 the railroad had been extended from Little Rock to Van Buren, shortening the length of the arduous journey. On June 8, 1881, university officials welcomed the arrival of the first train to Fayetteville from St. Louis. Newspaper accounts applauded the opening of the Frisco Railway, predicting prosperity and growth in Washington County. Ten thousand people turned out to greet the train at the depot. Nearly everyone associated with the university turned out to witness the event, including the university cadets and the Cadet Band leading a parade celebrating the momentous occasion. The train came in from the north that day, but in the next years railroad workers completed the rail line to Van Buren.

In 1881, the Military Department obtained one hundred dollars from the state legislature for a heating stove for use in the basement of University Hall, musical instruments, and other necessities deemed appropriate by the commandant.

Though there were less than one hundred college students on the campus in 1882 (with about an equal number of preparatory students), the Military Department continued as part of the curriculum with the twelve-member AIU Cornet Band proudly listed in the school's annual report. In fact the band is mentioned routinely in nearly all of the annual reports of AIU up until the end of the century, most often listing all of its members yearly by name.

During the commencement festivities of 1886, it was mentioned in an article in the June 6 issue of the *Arkansas Gazette* that "Gov. Hughes was cordially received by citizens, faculty and students. . . . The A.I.U. battalion (including) the Arkansas Industrial University band, served as escort from the depot to the (Van Winkle) hotel. The battalion, in full uniform, with bayonets glistening in the sunlight, never looked better as they stepped with manly grace and military tread to the swelling strains of the band."

The *Arkansas Gazette* noted in an article dated May 31, 1892, regarding the ceremony of decoration of the graves in the Confederate Cemetery in Fayetteville that "the band from the university rendered valuable assistance, and furnished splendid music. The university has reason to be proud of its band."

The earliest photo found of the AIU Cadet Band was printed in the 1892 "Catalogue and Report of the AIU" and is shown on page 11.

In 1894 John C. Futrall, in addition to serving as the president of the AIU, was the coach of the first football team on the campus. The team was named the Cardinals and played three games that year, decisively beating Fort Smith High twice and then losing big to Texas 54–0. There is no evidence that the Cadet Band of the university entertained at any of the games that year.

According to Harrison Hale in his history of the university, "one of the earliest out-of-town trips made by the band was to Little Rock on April 24, 1896, when it played at the Intercollegiate Oratorical Association Contest. . . ."

As far as can be ascertained, the Cadet Band remained at about twenty in number up until about 1905. Whether it was thought that that was as big a band the department needed or because that was how many instruments and uniforms that the Military Department found usable is unknown. An inventory by the Military Department in 1900 listed a set of band equipment for thirty.

In the first student yearbook, named the *Cardinal*, commemorating the 1897–98 school year, a studio photograph of the Cadet Band posing soberly staring at the camera appeared in the pages. Also all the names of the members and officers were listed. Thus began the yearbook recording of images of the university's Cadet Band.

FAYETTEVILLE.

Commencement Exercises—Decorating the Confederate Graves—Gov. Hughes.

Arkansas Gazette Correspondence.

FAYETTEVILLE, June 6, 1886.

As the time for commencement exercises of the University approaches, the town assumes a more stirring and popular aspect, the student becomes more enthusiastic, and numerous notables from various parts of the state may be seen about the lobby of the Van Winkle.

Gov. Hughes was cordially received by citizens, faculty and students last Friday.

The A. I. U. battalion, commanded by the worthy and proficient gentleman, Prof. Whitham, as commandant, aided by the handsome and popular young captains, Tillar and Bates, headed by the Arkansas Industrial University band, served as escort from the depot to the hotel. The governor was tendered a private cab and the escort conducted themselves with the usual military formality. The battalion, in full uniform, with bayonets glistening in the sunlight, never looked better as they stepped with manly grace and military tread to the swelling strains of the band.

The *Arkansas Gazette* article above notes the participation of the band at the 1886 commencement ceremony.

In the Eighth Catalogue of the AIU, members of the Cadet Band were first listed by name as noted below. The earliest photograph of the Cadet Band this author has been able to find was printed in the 1892 AIU Catalogue (note the band at the left of the battalion proper on the facing page). An accompanying paragraph states that

> in connection with the battalion there is a military band, which is composed of cadets, not to exceed twenty, who can perform on a band instrument, or who show an aptitude and desire to learn. The band receives the best instruction attainable, practices three times a week, and performs at all military ceremonies. The instruments are furnished by the government and are of the best make and most improved pattern.

Also listed in that report are officers and non-commissioned officers for the field, staff, and band including Frank Barr as chief musician and J. E. Kirkham as drum major. Frank Barr would later become the band's first faculty director. The armory of the Military Department was for years located in the "damp north wing of University Hall" with "two smaller rooms, adjacent to the main room, (that) provided space for storage of the band equipment." (Raymond Considine, "The History of the Military Education at the University of Arkansas," 1986)

Also note that in 1894, football began with John C. Futrall as the coach.

EIGHTH CATALOGUE

OF THE

Arkansas Industrial University,

LOCATED AT

FAYETTEVILLE, WASHINGTON COUNTY, ARKANSAS.

FOR YEAR ENDING JUNE 10th, 1880.

AND

ANNOUNCEMENT FOR 1880-81.

ORGANIZED SEPTEMBER 18th, 1871.

JUNE 1880.

LITTLE ROCK:
ARKANSAS DEMOCRAT PRINT.
1880.

A. I. U. Band.

W. E. MASSIE, *First Leader and Instructor.*

F. T. DAUGHERTY, *Second Leader.*

W. A. BRIANT, *First B Flat.*

W. HUDSON, *Second B Flat.*

R. E. L. VANWINKLE, *First Alto.*

C. K. CHANSLOR, *Second Alto.*

C. D. GREAVES, *First Tenor.*

B. M. BROWN, *Second Tenor.*

J. L. REINACH, *Baritone.*

H. STROUP, *Tuba.*

H. WELLS, *Bass Drum.*

F. BOTEFUHR, *Snare Drum.*

A BAND ON THE CAMPUS, 1874–1908

The AIU Cadet Band, 1897.
The first studio photograph of the Cadet Band was printed in the 1897 *Cardinal.* Twenty men are in the photo although twenty-eight cadets are named. A new football coach was hired in 1897; in fact six different men coached the team between 1897 and 1908 when the famed Hugo Bezdek took over.

The AIU Cadet Band, 1898.

Cadet Band, 1899–1900.
In the yearbook the members of a separate eight-man bugle corps were also listed by name. In 1899 the Arkansas Legislature voted to change the name of the Arkansas Industrial University to the University of Arkansas.

The University of Arkansas Cadet Band, 1900–1901.
The men in the upper insets are T. E. Sanders, first lieutenant, commanding band; M. R. Herron, first lieutenant, leader of band; and L. E. Worthley, second lieutenant, assistant leader of band.

Cadet Band, 1901–2. Bandmaster Frank Barr seated in bowler hat. Barr served as band-master until 1917.

Cadet Band, 1902–3. Most of the earliest photos of the band were taken by C. E. Watton, a Fayetteville photographer.

Cadet Band, 1903–4.

Many of the band photos for most of the next ten years were taken by Grabill Studios. (Note "Grabill" inscribed on the photos.)

The first campus newspaper, the *Ozark*, was begun on campus.

Cadet Band, 1904–5.

It is first mentioned in the 1905 *Cardinal* that the Cadet Band "aid[ed] the football and baseball managements in advertising their games."

Cadet Band and Trumpet Corps, 1905–6.

**Cadet Band and
Battalion, 1905–6.**
On parade with Carnall
Hall in the background.
In 1906 the *Ozark* was
retitled the *University
Weekly*.

A BAND ON THE CAMPUS, 1874–1908

Cadet Band, 1906–7.
On the steps of University Hall.

Trumpet Corps 1907–8.
Fourteen members were listed in the Cardinal.

Cadet Band 1907–8.
Bandmaster Barr standing by column at upper right.

uring the early 1900s the annual inspection remained a point of emphasis because it was the only means by which the War Department rated the institutions and their cadets. Generally scheduled on a Saturday early in the month of April, the format for the day's activities varied little until after 1916. In describing the inspection of 1908, the campus newspaper, the *University Weekly* reported that

> the Cadet Band assembled first, taking their positions to the extreme right of where the regiment would form. They sounded "Adjutant Call," which was the signal for the regiment to form. They followed with "To The Color" signaling the beginning of the inspection. After marching in review, the cadets formed a "Column of Companies" formation. At that time the inspector conducted the "in ranks" inspection, looking at the general appearance of the cadets, their rifles, and the band equipment. After this, the boys performed movements in regimental, battalion and company formations, concluding the day with a regimental parade led by the Cadet Band.

In 1909 the department added a new wrinkle, performing calisthenic exercises and rifle drills to music. The cadets conducted the dress parade and inspection on occasions when visiting dignitaries came to the school. Members from the legislature and the board of trustees usually visited at least once a year.

The years between the turn of the century and World War I brought increasing attention to the University of Arkansas Cadet Band and the school itself. Also, a sense of identity to the campus became more entrenched with the composition of both a varsity song (to be sung on into the twenty-first century as the alma mater) and a field song (the "Arkansas Fight Song" still heard at Arkansas sporting events). When the Confederate Soldiers held their great reunion in 1911, the band received a lot of publicity and press coverage when they traveled by train to Little Rock for the honor of leading Gen. John B. Gordan's division in the great parade and playing for other events over the three-day gathering. Then of course, there was the playing at the football games coached by the famous Hugo Bezdek. It was during this time the football team was renamed the "Razorbacks."

In 1916, the University of Arkansas officially became an institution authorized by the War Department to maintain a unit of the

CHAPTER 3

The Band Takes On New Responsibilities

1908–1921

senior division of the Reserve Officers Training Corps (ROTC). This new designation also brought about the eventual renaming of the Cadet Band as the University of Arkansas ROTC Razorback Band. Soon, with the United States becoming more involved in the war in Europe, the Student Army Training Corps (SATC) took over the ROTC Department, preparing more and more students to serve in the military. In the midst of it all, the band often participated in patriotic parades in and around Fayetteville and in campaigns for the selling of Liberty Bonds to support the war effort. But once the war came to an end, ROTC returned to its original mission on campus and the band to marching during drill maneuvers on the lawn in front of Old Main and at the occasional football game.

On the journalistic front the student campus paper, the *University Weekly,* underwent a name change in 1921 when its staff decided to publish two issues a week. The new name decided upon was the *Arkansas Traveler.*

Cadet Band, 1908–9.

The University of Arkansas Alma Mater

In the spring of 1909 a contest was held on campus for writing the lyrics to an alma mater (fifty dollars to the winner) which would be put to music by music professor Henry D. Tovey. Nineteen hundred and eight was also the first year of legendary coach Hugo Bezdek, after a series of short-term football coaches. Bezdek would also coach the baseball team.

The Winning Song

ALMA MATER

I.

Pure as the dawn on the brow of thy beauty
    Watches thy Soul from the mountains of God
Over the Fates of thy children departed
    Far from the land where their footsteps have trod.
Beacon of Hope in the ways dreary lighted:
    Pride of our hearts that are loyal and true;
From those who adore unto one who adores us—
    Mother of Mothers, we sing unto you.

II.

We, with our faces turned high to the Eastward,
    Proud of our place in the vanguard of Truth.
Will sing unto thee a new song of thanksgiving—
    Honor to God and the Springtime of Youth.
Shout of the victor or tear of the vanquished;
    Sunshine or tempest thy heart is e'er true;
Pride of the Hills and the white-laden Lowlands—
    Mother of Mothers, we kneel unto you.

III.

Ever the Legions of Sin will assail us,
    Ever the Battle in Cities afar;
Still in the depths will thy Spirit eternal
    Beckon us on like a piloting Star.
Down the dim years do thy dead children call thee,
    Wafted to Sleep while the Springtime was new;
We, of the Present, thy Hope of the Future—
    Mother of Mothers, we pray unto you.

The 1909–10 Cadet Band standing at attention behind the student officers and in front of the remainder of the battalion on the east lawn of University Hall. The band was also mentioned in the *University Weekly* as playing at football games and rallies.

Arkansas's 1909 football team went undefeated under the coaching of Hugo Bezdek. The record was 7-0 with two of their opponents canceling their games after Arkansas upset the heavily favored Oklahoma team. Toward the end of the season, Bezdek and others started referring to the team "as playing like scrappy razorbacks," and the nickname appeared in a few papers as such. In the spring the new mascot name appeared often in articles about the baseball team. And by the fall of 1910, the football team was being commonly referred to as the Razorbacks.

The University of Arkansas
Cadet Bugle Corps,
1909–10.

Cadet Band, 1910–11.
In May of 1911, the band traveled to Little
Rock for the Reunion of Confederate
soldiers held there and at Camp Shaver.
For three days the boys entertained the
veterans with official and impromptu
concerts and parades. Travel to and
from the reunion was by train.

Cadet Band, 1911–12.

Cadet Band 1912–13.
The Annual Inspection of Cadets was always a big day for the Military Department. In the spring of 1913 the event won praise for the 134 cadets by Capt. W. H. Raymond from Washington, D.C. The *University Weekly* noted that "the band was in good condition and by the good quality of music it produced, proved that it is one of the best organizations in the department."

When William Edwin Douglass (class of 1913) was an undergrad, he wrote the lyrics to a spirit song that he showed to his music teacher, Prof. Henry Tovey. Tovey later set the words to music and the tune still echoes throughout the Ozarks today as the "Arkansas Fight Song."

Cadet Band, 1913–14.

Cadet Band, 1914–15.
The *University Weekly* printed in an April issue that the Cadet Band played dirge music on the way to Evergreen Cemetery during a military funeral procession for the recently deceased Mrs. Gladson, wife of University of Arkansas vice president W. N. Gladson.

Cadet Band, 1915–16.

Left are photographs from the 1916 *Razorback* showing the Cadet Band and Battalion in a parade in Fort Smith prior to the playing of the Arkansas–Oklahoma State football game.

ROTC Band, 1916–17.
Frank Barr, the first faculty director of the U of A Band, resigned his position
following the 1916–17 school year.

Frank Barr, *Director*

University of Arkansas ROTC Band with Ben Winkleman (far right) as the new Bandmaster, 1917–18. Winkleman, also a star Razorback football player, was named team captain in 1921, and made the All-SWC teams in 1920 and 1921.

Although no picture is available showing the 1918–19 band, the *University Weekly* mentioned that the band did march in the Memphis Centennial Parade in May.

The University of Arkansas Military Band (as it was labeled in the 1920 *Razorback*) with Ben Winkleman, band leader, with baton at center. Among other activities, the band marched on campus in the annual Agri Day Parade.

Despite calls from some fans for the band to participate in more activities on campus or to create a new band separate from ROTC Band for non-military activities, Capt. Kenneth M. Halpine, head of ROTC, defended the band's priorities as first being with military drills and campus duties, and when time permitted, providing pep at athletic events. Lack of funds to create a new band soon made the point moot. No photos are available for the 1920–21 or 1921–22 bands, but articles about the group appeared during both years in the campus newspaper.

From 1921 until 1926, Owen C. Mitchell, a former University of Arkansas bandsman, served as the director of the ROTC Razorback Band and by all accounts was a very popular leader of the group. The powers-that-be in the Military Department at the university and the fans of the football team who wanted to see more "pep" exhibited at the games praised his efforts. During that time the very successful Francis Schmidt came on board as the new football coach, and he also introduced a men's basketball team to the campus and to the Southwest Conference.

Also in the interval covered by this chapter the university celebrated its fiftieth anniversary (called at the time its "semi-centennial"), the band started wearing more civilian-looking uniforms, including beanies, to the ballgames, and the first homecoming festivities were established on the campus. The band took regular trips to Little Rock by train to play at Arkansas football games, John Philip Sousa and his band played a special concert in the auditorium of University Hall, and Kappa Kappa Psi and Sigma Alpha Iota were established on the Fayetteville campus as music service fraternities.

For the school year 1921–22, the band acquired a new director—Owen C. Mitchell. The *Arkansas Traveler* reported that the band traveled by train to Fort Smith to support the football team in its victory against SMU (14–9). The Arkansas Boosters Club (ABC) raised the funds for the band's trip.

In June of 1922, the campus celebrated its semi-centennial. The celebration took place in 1922 rather than in 1921 because, although the school was established in 1871, students did not begin attending until January 1872.

In 1926, the ROTC Razorback Band found itself under the only conductor in its long history to have been a military bandmaster. He was Patrick F. Freyer, a retired band leader of the U. S. Army. He only held the position for one year, but he inaugurated an event never seen before on the university campus—the concert band performance. Up until that time, the ROTC Razorback Band had only performed as the adjunct to military parade events, athletic contests, or commencement exercises. He finally gave the band an opportunity to be the main event.

CHAPTER 4

The Razorback ROTC Band Makes an Impact

1921–1927

OWEN C. MITCHELL, *Director*

University of Arkansas ROTC Razorback Band, 1922–23.

Band members that year first wore more casual uniforms to athletic events as can be seen in the picture above (note the beanies). More conventional military duds were worn at ROTC events. With funds raised by the ABC the band traveled by train to Little Rock for the Arkansas-Rice game, played at Kavanaugh Field. Francis Schmidt began his very successful coaching career in the fall of 1922. Organized by the ABC, with C. G. "Crip" Hall as its president, Homecoming began as an annual event in the fall. Hall, onetime secretary of state for Arkansas, would continue to be part of the Homecoming activities on into the 1960s.

ROTC Razorback Band, 1923–24.

Two special events for the band occurred during the school year. First, John Philip Sousa led his famous band in a concert held in the auditorium of University Hall on February 6 to a packed house with many Razorback Band students in the audience. Sousa was a very proud member of the national Kappa Kappa Psi band fraternity, and coincidentally or not, the Lambda Chapter of the organization was established on campus later that spring. Also, Coach Schmidt started a men's basketball team on campus that began competing in the Southwest Conference.

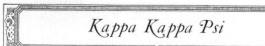

Kappa Kappa Psi

National Musical Fraternity
Established at Arkansas, 1924

MEMBERS

CLAUD SANFORD
GREER NICHOLS
LOYCE HATHCOCK
THOMAS DOUGLAS
RAYMOND AUSTIN
THURL BENBROOK

CARL TOALSON
NEUMAN LEIGHTON
ALFRED HATHCOCK
BRUCE BENNETT
AUBREY BABER
JOEL W. BLAKE

Top row—NICHOLS, BABER, TOALSON, BLAKE
Bottom row—L. HATHCOCK, LEIGHTON, A. HATHCOCK, DOUGLAS, BENBROOK

ROTC Razorback Band, 1924–25.

The 1925 *Razorback* included the following comments regarding the band:

> The band has played its part well during the year, speaking both literally and figuratively. On Thursdays its forty odd members appear in uniform with diverse military accoutrements and furnish music for the military ceremonials; at the games this same band presents itself in red and white Razorback fighting togs and does a substantial part in keeping up the true mountain swine fighting spirit. At pep meetings the band is right there; the band is available on Engineers' and Agri Days; it is available for sundry other festivals and celebrations. During the football season the band journeyed to Little Rock for the memorable Mississippi victory and to Fort Smith for the Phillips University game. Garbed in red and white the University of Arkansas Band partook in the annual Blossom Festival in Rogers and in the Rotary Convention at Fort Smith.

ROTC Razorback Band, 1925–26.

This year a woman tried out for the band for the first time and was accepted as a member. However, there is no evidence that she followed through with her enrollment.

ROTC Razorback Band, 1926–27.

The new school year brought a new band director to the ROTC Department. He was Patrick F. Freyer, a retired band leader of the U. S. Army. Addison L. Wall was in the second year of his three-year stint as student director of the band; it might be noted that he served under a different director each year. The band traveled to football games played against Hendrix in Little Rock and LSU in Shreveport. Both trips were funded by the ABC with proceeds from selling "tags"—spirit-boosting ribbons students wore proclaiming "Go Razorbacks" or "Beat (whatever team was being played)." In the spring, the first ever concerts presented by the Razorback Band were performed on February 16 and March 17 in the University Hall Auditorium to excellent reviews in the *Arkansas Traveler*. Both concerts were also broadcast live over the radio waves. The band also played for the Rotary Convention held in Tulsa and at the Strawberry Festival in Van Buren.

Patrick F. Freyer,
Band Director 1926–27.

Addison L. Wall,
Student Director 1925–28.

By the time that Francis Judah Foutz took over the conducting duties of the ROTC Razorback Band, the group had grown to seventy men in size and needed new uniforms to outfit the group. By performing concerts for a nominal charge and acquiring other substantial donations (one from the Athletic Department) Foutz was able to clad the group in new togs by the fall of 1928. Other innovations Foutz introduced during his long tenure with the Music Department were the Girls' Drum Corps (though short-lived), increased radio concerts, and the band's forming letters and other formations on the field at football halftime breaks. And though the band had traveled to out-of-state games previously, they became a more frequent occurrence during these years (most often to Texas, Louisiana, and Oklahoma).

Also this period covers the era of the stock market crash, the Great Depression, and the events that led up to World War II. Events on the University of Arkansas campus reflected the times with limestone buildings going up on campus as WPA projects, and more and more women attending the campus. The first woman was accepted into the band to play at football games, and Chi Omega built the Greek Theatre that would become a focal point for band activities for years to come.

As for the group's quarters, the band moved from the basement of University Hall to the basement of the Commerce Building and eventually acquired a building of its own on the side of the hill where Daniel E. Ferritor Hall currently stands. It was a time that also heralded legendary drum majors of the ROTC Razorback Band such as Norman "Jelly" Warnock, Harry "Snooks" Crumpler, and Jimmy Baker.

One of the great Razorback football coaches mentored the team during that time—Fred Thomsen. And a legend in Razorback basketball led the boys to a number of first place finishes in the SWC—Glen Rose.

Swing music took the country by storm, the band branched out at halftime shows with the latest in drill maneuvers (wheels, cakewalks, fan counter marches, and intertwining designs), and construction began on campus for a new football stadium designed to hold 13,500 fans.

In the fall of 1938, the ROTC Razorback Band took to the rails bound for California to play at the Arkansas–Santa Clara game and to help publicize along the way a new Paramount movie entitled

CHAPTER 5

The Foutz Years

1927–1940

Arkansas Traveler. Paramount Studios paid half of the band's expenses on the trip in return. The band also performed at the Arkansas-Villanova game played in 1939 in Philadelphia.

Bringing the Foutz chapter to a close in the fall of 1940, the director resigned on short notice citing poor health. Subsequently he left Fayetteville bound for California to recuperate.

The ROTC Razorback Band prepares to march through Fayetteville streets during 1927 Homecoming Parade.

Francis Judah Foutz.

The University of Arkansas ROTC Razorback Band, 1927–28.

The 1928 *Razorback* included the following paragraph about the band:

> At all the athletic contests the band turned out whether it was football, basketball or even track. The unusual pep that was displayed at the basketball games was due largely to the band. Of course, they went to Little Rock and helped "Beat Hendrix," and while there played four concerts at the Palace Theatre. Not to be forgotten are the parades which the band led, Homecoming, as well as the regular Thursday drill parades. To Addison Wall goes the credit of starting a drive for new red and white uniforms for the band; something the boys have sadly needed for more than a year. The Little Rock concerts, as well as concerts given at the Ozark and at Springdale, were given in order that next year the boys would be partly rewarded by snappy new uniforms. When spring came, Sunday afternoon concerts were given on the campus.

Also in the spring of 1928 Foutz created the new Girls' Drum Corps made up of about twenty female U of A students.

ROTC Razorback Band, 1928–29.

The new uniforms for the band to wear at athletic events finally arrived in the fall of 1928. The accessories included special hats and shirts plus a distinctive red and white cape. For military events, the band wore the uniforms pictured at left.

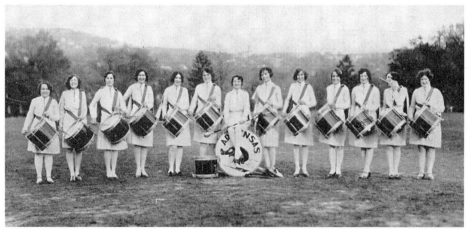

The Girls Drum Corps was featured in the 1929 *Razorback* with Rachel Bacus as drum major.

Francis Schmidt resigned after the 1928–29 school year following two final winning seasons in football (8-1 and 7-2) and four consecutive seasons being number 1 in the Southwest Conference in basketball (season records of 23-2, 14-2, 19-1 and 19-1).

The Razorback Band and the Girls' Drum Corps are shown performing together during a halftime presentation on the U of A gridiron in the fall of 1928. Although there was a valiant effort to maintain the Girls' Drum Corps as a unit, there is no evidence that the group continued after the 1929–30 school year.

Very popular on the University of Arkansas campus were dance bands. Frequently playing at student and fraternity dances was former Razorback Band director Owen C. Mitchell's Arkansas Travelers Orchestra pictured left (Mitchell is at the piano). Another such group was the Globe Trotters Orchestra. Both dance bands included Razorback Band members in their rosters and were featured in the 1929 *Razorback*.

The University of Arkansas ROTC Razorback Band 1929–30

The following is from the 1930 *Razorback* regarding the band:

A regular part of the Band season is spent in the preparation and playing of several concerts and an ever-increasing selection of radio numbers. There are also the calls for the Band to play in other towns for special events, such as the opening of the civic auditorium in Eureka Springs, the Agri Parade, Hospitality and Trade Days, Fort Smith events, and often occasions at Tulsa, Oklahoma.

The band has continued its practice of forming letters at football games between halves, a custom started last year. A number of trick and fancy formations have also been used with great success, but only after hours of practice. The closest cooperation possible is maintained between the Band, The Girls' Drum Corps, the Rootin' Rubes, and the Arkansas Boosters Club. Highlights for the Band in the 1929 football season were the forming of letters and the march between halves at the Homecoming as well as the Texas games. Both visiting teams brought bands with them.

Two football trips were made by the Band, one to the Louisiana game at Shreveport and one to Stillwater Thanksgiving for the Oklahoma A & M game. Both trips were successful with the Band cheering Arkansas on to victory . . .

The Band is divided into two divisions, one the official ROTC Band that plays at all parades and is present on all military occasions, the other the pep band which plays at athletic contest and other events. The ROTC Band wears the regulation Army uniform supplied by the government. The other section of the band is smaller, only the best of the ROTC Band being a part of it. Special uniforms, purchased in 1928, are worn, and the Band makes a flashy appearance when clad in them.

The ROTC Razorback Band is shown at right taking the field in Fayetteville at halftime in the fall of 1929. The new football coach was Fred Thomsen, who would be in that position for thirteen seasons, and the new basketball coach was Charles Bassett, who would hold court for four years.

ROTC Razorback Band, 1930–31.

In 1930, Norman "Jelly" Warnock was selected as drum major of the band and served in that role until the spring of 1935. The Pep Band played at all the home football games that season plus traveling to Little Rock for the Texas A & M tilt, to Tulsa for the Tulsa game, and to Shreveport for the annual LSU game played in conjunction with the Louisiana State Fair. In addition, the band played at all the home basketball games played in Fayetteville. Note that the left picture of the band was taken in the newly completed Chi Omega Greek Amphitheatre.

The Razorback Band in the stands at a home game in Fayetteville. An incentive to retain juniors and seniors in the band (male students were only required to have two years of ROTC credit) was offered in selecting ten upperclassmen to receive refunds of $4.50 off activity fees and a $5.00 bonus cash payment. Also good news came to the ROTC Department when the U. S. Army donated $5,000.00 worth of new instruments and a large library of new music to the band program.

ROTC Razorback Band, 1931–32.

Written by former students of the University of Arkansas, the song shown on the following pages became a nationally recorded hit on radio, and an arrangement of it was played by the Razorback Band at some ballgames during the year. In the spring of 1932 John Philip Sousa died and the Lambda Chapter of Kappa Kappa Psi gave special recognition to the famous bandmaster at their May induction of new members.

Razorback* Rootin' Song
(University of Arkansas)

Words by
JEWELL HUGHES '15
and CATHARINE WALKER '30

Tune Ukulele
G C E A

Music by
WILLIAM M. PAISLEY '26

Con Spirito

1. I'm a
2. I'll root

slim old pig And I'm not so big And I live in the
out the rest For the Team that's best That is wear - ing the

O - zark hills. But I love to roam Far a-
Red and White And its such a thrill To be

way from home Just to give and to get some thrills.
root - in' still For the team has the pep all right.

Ukulele Arrangement by
Roy Smeck

* A Razorback is a lean-bodied, half-wild hog, found in the southern part of the United States. It is a nickname used for University of Arkansas athletes.

2

ROTC Razorback Band, 1932–33.

One of the largest bands on the campus to date, the group listed seventy-seven members in the 1933 *Razorback*. Having moved from the basement of University Hall to the basement of the Commerce Building a few years previously, in 1932 the band remodeled its quarters with new wall murals provided by the Art Department. Though the band participated at all the home football games and traveled to some of the away games, the team only won one of its tilts in the fall, losing six and tying the other two.

The University of Arkansas Band in its Football Band uniforms (above) and traditional ROTC uniforms (below), 1933–34. Notably during the fall semester Dr. Henry D. Tovey, head of the Music Department, professor, and composer of the alma mater and "Arkansas Fight Song," died in a Little Rock hospital of a cerebral hemorrhage. He had been chair of the Music Department for twenty-five years.

FOLLOWING THE BAND AROUND — A study in shadows from atop a telephone pole . . . The band leads out in perfect formation in the Little Rock parade . . . Master Warnock entertains Louisiana State Fair visitors . . . Maestro Foutz takes charge . . . We follow the band through the streets of Tulsa . . . Arkansas musicians made a big hit at the Tulsa game . . . but shared honors with Fort Smith band members Homecoming.

The photos on this page document a couple of the football trips the band took in 1933 (printed in the 1934 *Razorback* with original captions). The team improved to 7-3 that year and played Centenary on January 1 in the Dixie Classic Bowl in Dallas. The basketball team finished the year under a new coach, Glen Rose, with a record of 16-8.

ROTC Razorback Band, 1934–35.

In addition to performing for all of the football games played in Fayetteville, the band traveled by train to the SMU game in Dallas, the Baylor game in Little Rock, and the Tulsa game in Tulsa. Tag sales sponsored by the ABC raised funds to allow the band to make those trips.

Band members arrive in Tulsa via train.

"Jelly" Warnock and his cousin "Snooks" Crumpler lead the band during the Homecoming Parade.

ROTC Razorback Band, 1935–36.
Sixty-one members made up the military unit of the band of whom fifty-two were chosen for the Athletic Pep Band.

A fifty-third member of the Pep Band was Earlene Upchurch, a bell lyre player from Fort Smith who was the first female on record to play in the band. Typically, she would stand in the middle of band members circled around her and play "Stardust" to their accompaniment. An emergency appendectomy limited her performances to only one season.

Harry Crumpler, who had acceded to the drum major position on the graduation of his cousin Jelly Warnock, became quite well known across the south for his acrobatic and skilled twirling exhibitions during games. His abilities with a baton inspired the director of the SMU band to invite Crumpler to front the Mustang Band in its appearance at the 1936 Rose Bowl Game and Parade; he stole the show.

The 1936–37 University of Arkansas ROTC Razorback Pep Band typically marched at half-time on the campus football field located at the time on the current Arkansas Union Plaza. Nearby on the current Ferritor Hall site, construction was beginning on a new band building with materials gleaned from the razing of the old Physics Building. Also there were plans and even auditions held for a twenty-member chorus to back up the marching band during halftime shows in 1936, but it did not material-ize. The band did travel by train to games played against LSU in Shreveport, Tulsa in Tulsa, SMU in Dallas, and Texas in Little Rock.

ROTC Razorback Band 1937–38.

Although only fifty-six men appear in the ROTC Band photo, seventy-two members' names were listed in the 1938 *Razorback*. The Pep Band included a new instrument in the fall—a "grid-organ" mounted on a chassis of a Model T Ford. Ethel Betty Williams performed at the console in civilian dress and played solos and with the band during games.

The Razorback Pep Band plays spiritedly from the stands. The musical repertoire expanded in 1937 to include more swing and popular numbers such as "Basin Street Blues," "Margie," and Duke Ellington's "Caravan" along with the traditional marches. The Concert Band also presented a series of concerts in the spring on campus, including one featuring the noted guest marimbist Clair Musser.

Candid photos from the 1939 *Razorback* focused on the Pep Band playing in the stands and drum major Judge Chapman leading the band in a tune.

The new University of Arkansas football stadium with seating available for 13,500 was completed and dedicated in 1938 as a WPA project on the site of the current field. The stadium was named for the sitting-governor Carl Bailey. After he was defeated in his bid for re-election in 1940 the stadium was thereafter referred to as Razorback Stadium.

The photo at left shows band members en route to California for the Santa Clara game played in San Francisco. Paramount Studios paid for much of the band's trip expenses in exchange for the band playing in movie theaters and parades along the way between Arkansas and California to promote the studio's new movie release, *Arkansas Traveler*. The band also traveled by train to football games played against Texas in Little Rock and Ole Miss in Memphis.

Kappa Kappa Psi

Local Chapter Is The Eleventh Of Thirty-Eight Attempting To Improve University Bands

Lambda Chapter of Kappa Kappa Psi band fraternity celebrated fifteen years of service to the band in the spring of 1939.

Row 1—Baker, Burton, Edwards, Fitton, Gitchel, Hill.
Row 2—Martin, Morrison, Pearce, Stuettgen, Waller, Witherspoon.

Head drum major Jimmy Baker (left) led the band in 1939, assisted by Raymond Jackson and Jack Joyce. John Grissom, a trombone player, came from the ranks on occasion to join in an occasional twirling exhibition.

U of A Pep Band members mug for the camera of a 1940 *Razorback* photographer. New Tyrolean Alpine uniforms paid for by special fundraising concerts in previous years were worn by the band in the fall of 1939. As an experiment, the first Band Day was held on campus early in the fall of 1939 when six area high-school bands from Missouri and Arkansas were invited to watch and perform at the Arkansas–Texas Christian University game played in Razorback Stadium.

Cheerleaders Albert Gannaway, Will Etta Long (more popularly known in later years as Willie Oates, the Hat Lady), and Fred Harrison lead the red-clad Razorback Band through downtown Little Rock in a pre-game parade in the fall of 1940. Articles in the *Arkansas Traveler* frequently referred to the Pep Band as the Razorback Drill Band.

Francis Judah Foutz (left in the above photo), the Razorback Band's director since 1927, resigned in November of 1940 because of ill health. Student director Gene Witherspoon (later to become the legendary director of the Arkansas Tech band) took over the conducting duties for the remainder of the semester until Robert Winslow was named the new director in January of 1941.

To keep the 1940 fall term on track for the band in the wake of Foutz's resignation, student director Gene Witherspoon, upon President J. William Fulbright's approval, led the ROTC Razorback Band through its paces until Robert Winslow came into the faculty as the new director in the spring of 1941.

Though the band performed well in the fall of 1941, the bombing of Pearl Harbor in December thinned the band's ranks considerably with men enlisting in the various branches of the armed forces. As the war continued to escalate and civilian men became scarcer on campus, Winslow opened the ranks to women in the Concert Band, a la musical Rosie the Riveters. And with the rails and major transportation systems given priority because of the war effort, band trips to out-of-town athletic events were suspended until after the war.

Eventually, the campus became an encampment for the Army Air Corps for specialized instruction in military and civilian industrial vocational employment. With such soldiers on campus, many of whom could play musical instruments, the ROTC Razorback Band combined efforts with the soldiers for Aircrew-ROTC concerts for a period. They even marched together as a unit at football games played in Razorback Stadium during the fall of 1943.

In 1943 Winslow took a leave of absence to complete his doctorate in music education, and Merton Zahrt was hired for the interim year. When Winslow returned in the summer of 1944, he only stayed on until 1945, leaving in the middle of the fall semester. To tide the band over until spring, the band director of Fayetteville High School, R. W. Willis, pulled double duty for the ROTC Razorback Band. In the spring of 1946, Dr. Merton Zahrt (having just completed his doctorate) returned as the university's band director and remained in that position until the end of the spring semester 1948.

During the above musical-chairs action of the Razorback Band director's position, the band frequently played for War Bond rallies and marched in patriotic parades around the town square and through the streets of Fayetteville.

By the time that the war ended in Europe and in the Pacific, almost everyone was anxious to get back to life as normal as possible. But normal for the university would never be the same. Soldiers descended en masse upon the school as beneficiaries of the G. I. Bill,

CHAPTER 6

The War Years and the Emergence of the Civilian Marching Razorback Band

1941–1948

and housing shortages and cramped classrooms required many temporary buildings to be transferred to and/or built on and near campus.

The return of soldiers to campus also pushed the dual role of the ROTC Razorback Band playing for military and athletic events to the eventual decision of creating separate bands for each function. Many returning ex-servicemen wanted to play in the athletic band, but did not want to play for ROTC activities. Hence, the creation of two officially separate bands on the campus (though a number of men played in both). And with the barrier having been broken for women playing in the band during the war, a number of women took advantage of later joining the Razorback Band during football, basketball, and concert seasons. They even marched as majorettes behind drum major J. P. "Pee Wee" Crumpler in front of the band during parades.

The University of Arkansas ROTC Razorback Band, spring 1941.

Although only forty-nine men appeared in the 1941 *Razorback* photo above, sixty-four members were listed as being enrolled in the group. Of that number fifty-four marched in the Razorback Drill Band. In the spring over sixty-five members were mentioned as playing in the Concert Band for a series of concerts performed on campus and in Rogers, Arkansas.

Even prior to the bombing of Pearl Harbor in December of 1941, there was a heightened awareness of the ROTC members' responsibilities on campus because of the escalating war in Europe. But there was still an excitement for Razorback football games as these pictures taken on the

trip to the Texas A & M game played in Little Rock reflect. The photo above right was taken at a rally in the Marion Hotel, and the one at the lower right features Bitsy Mullins on trumpet at the game. The bottom left photo taken on the return trip reflects the fact that Arkansas lost the game.

Mr. Winslow's boys at a game in the fall of 1941 wearing full-dress uniforms as opposed to the more informal Tyrolean Alpine attire.

Director Robert Winslow served as the director of the University of Arkansas Bands from 1941 until the early fall of 1945 save for the 1943–44 school year when he took leave to complete his doctorate at Columbia University.

The University of Arkansas ROTC Razorback Band posed in front of the Band Building for a photo in the 1942 *Razorback*. Entrance to the building was deceptive in that a long covered walkway attached to it allowed entry from ground to the second floor, while the downstairs first floor was built down the side of the hill.

The Varsity Club swing band led by Albert Gannaway (pictured above from the 1942 *Razorback*) was one of the most popular music groups on the U of A campus, playing at dinner dances, formals, sweater hops, and other gigs since 1935. Though the draft took its toll on its numbers (it had to be disbanded between 1943 and 1945), the group rebounded later and became a mainstay on campus until the early 1950s.

Male students from the Razorback Concert Band and the Basketball Pep Band were signing up for the military in droves, resulting in Winslow's pleas for women musicians to join the band as full-fledged members.

Following the 1941–42 football season Fred Thomsen resigned his coaching position after four consecutive losing seasons and joined the army as a captain. After the 1941–42 basketball season Glen Rose also quit his job, but on a more positive note. In the first of his last two seasons his boys were undefeated in SWC play and made it to the second round of the NCAA Tournament. Rose's final season saw a 19-4 record and a tie for first place in the Southwest Conference.

The photo of the Razorback Band above from the 1943 *Razorback* shows the group in their Tyrolean Alpine uniforms with women present for the first time as regular members. The women did not march at the football games but were invited to play in the Concert Band and at the basketball games. With more men leaving school to join the serv-

ices, frequent requests from Winslow were made for women to join the band. Not surprisingly, the band made no out-of-town trips to football games for the fall seasons from 1942 and 1944. A. F. Thomas, with baton in front row, served as drum major for 1941 and 1942.

ROTC Razorback Band, 1943–44.

Director Robert Winslow took leave for a year to finish his doctoral degree and Merton Zahrt, from the Eastman School of Music, served for the interim. One name that was listed in the *Razorback* as being a member of the band that year was Dale Bumpers, who later served as governor of and U. S. senator from Arkansas; he also was drum major for the better part of the fall of 1943 before joining the military in November.

Beginning in 1942 until the end of the war in 1945, an Army Air Corps unit used the university as a training area for specialized instruction in numerous vocational areas, both for military and for civilian industrial employment to support the war effort. Men in this program would come to the university for three to six months of specific academic instruction and then be flown out for military training on Army Air Corps posts across the country. Every month or so, a new group of men would arrive, and another would leave. The Army Air Corps unit had from twelve hundred to as many as two thousand men at any one time and became the most prominent group on the campus during that period. A number of men in the Air Corps could play instruments and were formed into what was known as the University Aircrew Band (its number of members obviously fluctuated), and Mr. Winslow and Mr. Zahrt served as their directors. As can be seen right, the Air Corps and campus ROTC Bands combined efforts marching before the Homecoming audience in 1943.

The Aircrew and ROTC Razorback Bands also combined their efforts to present a series of concerts on campus during the World War II years. Evidence of the dominating presence of the military at the school at the time can be seen in the right photo at a concert where both the band and the audience were awash in khaki.

As in the previous two years, the 1944–45 ROTC Razorback Band did not travel to any away football games. But it did continue to perform with members of the Air Corps band at home games in traditional drills wearing regulation uniforms. The band also played at local rallies in the support of selling War Bonds.

Having completed requirements for his doctorate, Winslow returned to the university, relieving Zahrt of his duties.

The University of Arkansas Razorback Bandsmen—and women—in the fall of 1945. Dr. Robert Winslow started the fall term continuing as director of the band, but by the middle of October he had turned in his resignation. Merton Zahrt, who by that time had completed his doctorate, was rehired for the job on a permanent basis. Dr. Zahrt could not be released from his faculty duties he had begun at Dennison University in Granville, Ohio, until the end of the fall term, so R. W. Willis (far right in above photo), the director of the Fayetteville High School Band, filled in until that time. Student director, Hartman Hotz, was a most valuable assistant to Mr. Willis during the interim. Also, it should be noted that women were finally allowed to march at football games. J. P. "Pee Wee" Crumpler (at left in photo) served as drum major.

ROTC Razorback Band, 1945–46.

It was not until the second semester of 1945–46 that great numbers of soldiers began returning from the war to enroll at the University of Arkansas. As a result the football band of 1945 was still relatively small in number, but they did travel to the game played in Tulsa for their first away game since the Tulsa game of 1941. In the spring of 1946, Dr. Zahrt and Kenneth Osborne, head of the Fine Arts Department, toured music departments of area high schools in an attempt to recruit new band and music students for the university.

ROTC Razorback Band, 1946–47.

By the fall of 1946 enrollment at the University of Arkansas was up considerably with the football band's ranks increasing from forty-five to eighty-five with only sixty-nine marching at games during halftime due to a shortage of uniforms.

From looking at the photo above only twenty-three of the listed thirty-two ROTC Razorback Band members showed up for their appearance in the 1947 *Razorback*.

In the fall of 1946, the football band picked up steam in traveling to out-of-town games including the ones against Ole Miss in Memphis, Rice in Little Rock, and LSU in the Cotton Bowl in Dallas on January 1 (which ended in a 0–0 tie). Back on campus on January 22, 1947, the Concert Band played a concert celebrating the seventy-fifth anniversary of the University of Arkansas (shown left). Also playing a series of concerts on campus throughout the remainder of the spring, things appeared to be getting back to "normal."

By the fall of 1947, the new uniforms, which should have been delivered for the previous season, finally arrived and the band strutted its stuff in the dark-red wool attire trimmed with silver braid and white crossed chest webbing worn above for the Homecoming Parade.

Mona Lee Morris and Patsy Poland (at left) were the band's first female twirlers, and they joined drum major J. P. Crumpler and fellow twirler Lawrence Kelley in fronting the band during parades and halftime shows.

The University of Arkansas Razorback Band after a concert in the Field House, spring 1948. Dr. Merton Zahrt is standing at the rear center in shirt and tie. Many returning soldier-musicians did not want to join the ROTC Band, but they wanted to join a civilian band at the university. As a result, the two bands became completely separate entities with a common director and a number of the male students belonging to both bands. Women were not allowed to play in the ROTC Band, but they were eagerly welcomed into the Razorback Band.

The above photo was taken as the Razorback Band marched down Dickson Street during Homecoming in 1947. Note the soldiers lining both sides of the street as the band passes. The Razorback football team under Coach John Barnhill won an opportunity at season's end to play William and Mary in the Dixie Bowl on January 1 in Birmingham. But the band did not accompany the team because the American Legion, sponsors of the game, selected their own drum and bugle corps to take charge of the halftime festivities.

CHAPTER 7

The Marty-Widder Years

1948–1956

After the resignation of Merton Zahrt, the hunt for a new band leader led to a man named Edmund J. Marty, more popularly known by his initials, E. J.

E. J. Marty was a consummate professional in self-promotion and public relations. During his seven years as director of the Razorback Band, he sent out frequent press releases regarding every action the band was going to take and then followed up with others about what it did once an event or activity was over. He seldom let an opportunity pass that could garner attention for the band. Some of this may have been the result of his upbringing and background. When he was a child, his parents, both professional musicians, moved to Baraboo, Wisconsin, which was the winter quarters for the Ringling Brothers Circus. His father played with the circus band in his off-hours, and his mother taught violin and piano. It was said that "Marty ogled the animals and began studying the piano."

Marty graduated from Lawrence College Music Conservatory and then went to Northwestern for his master's. Married to Ruth Fussner, Marty had previously taught at the University of Idaho, owned part interest in a music store, and taught private lessons on the French horn before he was offered the position of director of bands at the University of Arkansas. "The challenge was too great," Marty said, so he took the job. His responsibilities included directing both the Razorback Marching Band and the ROTC Band.

Among the innovations and firsts that Marty introduced to the Marching Razorback Band was the selection of the first female as a drum major for the group, a talented and award-winning twirler, Jeannine Hartley, who led the band on the field for three years. While Marty was at the University of Arkansas, the band grew from seventy-five to one hundred members enabling the band to take on the moniker of the Marching 100 (and at times calling themselves the Thunderin' 100). In addition to football and basketball game appearances, Marty also concentrated on the Concert Band and smaller ensemble work with the brass, woodwind, and percussion sections. Furthermore, he held a series of concert tours across Arkansas, promoting and recruiting for the university band program. To encourage and reward the students for excellence in performance and service to the band, an awards system was created, and those awards were handed out in the first ever Annual Awards Banquet in 1951. And the band obtained its first official Voice of the Razorback Band with Lewis Epley Jr. in 1954. Plus, the group added a calliope to its instrumentation along the way.

During Marty's tenure, War Memorial Stadium was completed and dedicated, and the football team played its first televised SWC game under the lights at night (in Fort Worth). Also, besides marching at the Little Rock and Fayetteville football games, the band made regular marching appearances in the Arkansas Livestock Show Parade in Little Rock and was the band of honor in the most prestigious Mardi Gras Parade in New Orleans in 1949. In July of 1954 the band performed for the International Lion's Club Convention in New York City. Tau Beta Sigma, the national band service sorority, established itself at the U of A, and plans were laid out for a nationally broadcast radio program on the campus with the Razorback Band as its star. Time constraints on the students and a lack of scholarship compensation for the students involved caused Marty to back out of the radio deal.

During his years at the U of A, Marty pushed hard for more scholarships and/or fee waivers for band members and requested a better physical plant and bigger budget so the band could grow. He also appealed for a full-time assistant to help with administrative matters. His part-time assistant, Roger Widder, had other duties as a woodwind instructor in the Music Department that took most of his time. By August of 1955, Marty and the university administration parted ways when the school did not meet his demands.

Ironically when Roger Widder agreed to become the interim band director for 1955–56, the university hired a full-time assistant, Lloyd Schmidt, to help him with the group. Widder took over for only one year, but as he told this author, "the (band members) knuckled down and gave me the best they had."

Marty and Widder led the Razorback Band during a period of great growth and spirit with the organization and their tenures paralleled those of four football coaches (John Barnhill, Otis Douglas, Bowden Wyatt, and Jack Mitchell) and three basketball coaches (Eugene Lambert, Presley Askew, and Glen Rose).

A new director for the Razorback Band was hired in 1948—Edmund J. Marty (more often known as E. J.). He came to the U of A with degrees from Lawrence College and Northwestern. Although Marty was director of both the Razorback and ROTC Bands, the two organizations continued to exist as completely separate units. New to the Razorback Band was the first woman ever chosen as its drum major—Jeannine Hartley, a former champion high-school twirler. Also in the front line were six majorettes and a featured male twirler, Larry Kelly, who was also drum major of the ROTC Band (below).

The 1948 Razorback Marching Band played at three football games in Fayetteville and four in Little Rock, including the game in which the newly completed War Memorial Stadium was dedicated. The group also traveled to Fort Worth, becoming the first band ever to be televised in a night game when the Razorbacks played TCU. All travel was by bus rather than in trains of previous years. Due to a shortage of uniforms only seventy-five members marched at games although a number of other musicians joined during concert season.

The Razorback Band played in small combos and at full strength at basketball games according to the 1949 yearbook. Featured at some of the games was Bill Compton on tympani accompanied by five herald trumpeters and five trombones playing the *Weinberger Concerto for Tympani and Brass.* During the spring of 1949, the Concert Band gave several concerts on campus and in surrounding communities.

With the ordering of more uniforms, the Razorback Band was able to suit up almost one hundred members during the fall of 1949. Playing at the Little Rock and Fayetteville football games, the band also traveled to Dallas for the SMU tilt.

Perhaps the highlight of the year was marching in the Mardi Gras Parade in New Orleans behind the king's float, the most prestigious position a band could hold. Special fundraising efforts organized by Director Marty and student leaders (left to right in bottom photo) Mike Sand, Jeannine Hartley, Alex Hamilton, John Fortenberry, and Bill Compton were required to make the trip a reality. The middle photo was taken by a band member within the ranks in the Mardi Gras parade. Note the King Rex float in front of the band.

Again leading the band in 1949, drum major Jeannine Hartley shared twirling duties with Pat Moore, Mary Ann Maddox, Franklin Ault (who also served as drum major for the ROTC Band, pictured below), Alice Aumick, and Mary Wise.

THE MARTY-WIDDER YEARS, 1948–1956

During E. J. Marty's (right) tenure as director
of the Razorback Band, Roger Widder (above)
served as his assistant director. Widder was also
a woodwind faculty member of the university's
Music Department, which required more
and more of his time as the years progressed.
Eventually, Widder's departmental responsibilities overshadowed his ability to be of much
assistance to Marty.

In the fall of 1950, the Razorback Band marched in a pregame parade beginning in North Little Rock and crossing a bridge over the Arkansas River into Little Rock. The band traveled by bus to Little Rock for three football games that season and to Fort Worth for the TCU game, the only out-of-state trip taken. Otis Douglas was the new Razorback football coach in 1950 and led the team to a lackluster 2-8 record.

Band members load up buses for yet another game away from Fayetteville. Overseeing the process was W. S. "Pop" Gregson (at left), a university faculty member who was the band's chief campus advocate from 1919 until he retired from the school in the fall of 1953.

The Razorback Band takes to the field in the above 1951 *Razorback* photo marching downfield in a showboat formation complete with a paddlewheel.

Band president for 1950–51 John Watson, drum major Jeannine Hartley, and assistant director Roger Widder go over halftime show plans with band director Marty (bottom right).

Tau Beta Sigma, the national band service sorority, joined Kappa Kappa Psi on the U of A campus in the fall of 1950. Original members included Rose Marie Rapier, Jeannine Hartley, Jean McIntyre, Patricia Moore, Vivian Jorgensen, and Rebecca Sheeks above with Mrs. E. J. Marty (at extreme left) serving as the sponsor of Psi Chapter.

Participants in the 1950 Homecoming festivities included a card section in the stands, the ninety-member Razorback Band in the center of the field and the white-helmeted Pershing Rifle Team flanking the band. Also present was a mixed chorus singing a special number commemorating the fact that it was also Armistice Day.

The left photo provides a rare glimpse into what was the rehearsal hall in the Band Building in the early 1950s. Note the terraced rows and support post in the center of the room. In addition to performing at basketball games, band members also performed concerts on campus as part of the Concert Band, as well as participating in the spring campus carnival, GAEBALE. (The name came from the first letters of the seven colleges on campus then: Graduate, Arts and Sciences, Education, Business, Agriculture, Law, and Engineering.) In May of 1951, the band held its first annual Awards Banquet at the UARK Bowl where special service awards were presented to deserving band members.

The fall of 1951 saw the Razorback Band performing at all the Little Rock and Fayetteville football games plus traveling to Dallas for the SMU tilt. Above, the new drum major, Tommy Gray (a graduate of the Navy School of Music and six-year Navy Band veteran) leads the band through the streets of Little Rock during a pregame parade. At Little Rock games that fall, the band performed a number of halftime shows illuminated only by caplights (battery-operated penlights inserted where the plumes were normally placed) while the stadium lights were dimmed.

On Dad's Day 1951 at the Texas-Arkansas game in Fayetteville, the Razorback Band also gave a nod to "M-O-M" with the above formation. Note that there are no majorettes in the photo. Marty announced at the beginning of the season that the twirlers would only be used for "parades and related affairs" during the year. He was quoted in the *Traveler,* saying, "the majorettes are often used to 'cover up' any lack of skill the band itself might contain." He also said that "a band should stand or fall on its own intrinsic marching and playing value." The majorettes did perform at the Santa Clara game played in Little Rock that year. And in subsequent seasons, as a result of public pressure, the girls returned to performing regularly at football games.

Band members show their exuberance aboard a bus en route to an out-of-town game.

For away games that the band was not able to attend, members both sent the football team off and welcomed them back home with a musical bang.

Marty and Razorback Band members back up the U of A cheerleaders at a pep rally "Calling the Hogs" in the lobby of Little Rock's Marion Hotel. There was considerable discussion throughout the fall of 1951 about Marty and the Razorback Band hosting a nationally broadcast radio program. But the whole idea fell through when Marty insisted that the band be compensated thousands of dollars in scholarship money for the students who would be required to do the work.

Toward the end of the 1951 football season, Marty procured an old-fashioned calliope which made its debut during halftime at Homecoming. Marty's parents had worked for Ringling Brothers Circus when he was a child, which may have sparked his interest in making it part of the band's shows. The calliope was also used for stunts and entertainment performed at basketball games.

In addition to performing at GAEBALE in the spring of 1952, the Concert Band also presented a few well-received concerts in the newly completed Fine Arts Concert Hall and a series of Twilight Concerts on the lawn in front of Old Main.

The Razorback Band received new uniforms in the fall of 1952 and proudly wore them during the first pep rally of the season in the Greek Theatre as pictured above. Also at the first home game, the band continued a tradition which had begun a few years earlier inviting area high-school bands to participate in Band Day at the university. Eighteen bands showed up.

Note the white coveralls worn by band members above. Those were pep rally and traveling uniforms for the Razorback Band.

Band members (right) mug for the camera on the way to a football game played in Little Rock's War Memorial Stadium.

In addition to playing at Little Rock and Fayetteville football games, the Razorback Band was also on hand at the Arkansas-TCU game played in Fort Worth in 1952. Shown left is the band playing a pep rally in the Hotel Marion prior to one of the Little Rock games.

Homecoming 1952 was a celebrated affair in Fayetteville with the Arkansas Band spelling out "A-L-U-M" on the field while the card section formed "U-A" in the stands. The football team lost the game against SMU 27–17 and later finished the season as it had in 1950 with a 2-8 record.

At the Ole Miss game in Little Rock in 1952, the Razorback majorettes dressed up like characters from the "Pogo" comic strip during the halftime show. The cartoon's creator, Walt Kelly shown with the majorettes at right, was a guest at the game.

Included in the concerts given by the Concert Band in the spring of 1953 was a benefit performance for the polio ward of the Washington County Hospital, which the band is shown rehearsing for in the band hall.

In the fall of 1953 the Razorback Band's ranks had finally grown to one hundred members prompting E. J. Marty to rename the group The Razorback Marching 100 (it was also at times dubbed The Thunderin' Hundred). In the left photo the Marching 100 lined up in a flying wedge for the fanfare at halftime of the Ole Miss game played in Memphis.

Band members return to Fayetteville from the long trip to Memphis after the 28–0 defeat at the hands of the Ole Miss Rebels. The charter Crown Coaches became the band's home away from home.

The aptly labeled charter bus is provided an escort from Morrilton to Little Rock by the Arkansas State Police. In 1953 the Arkansas football team welcomed a new coach, Bowden Wyatt, but suffered through a 3-7 season.

The Razorback Marching 100 sounds the alma mater for Homecoming 1953. W. S. "Pop" Gregson, chaperone and guardian angel over the band since 1919, retired because of health reasons just a couple of weeks prior to the Homecoming game.

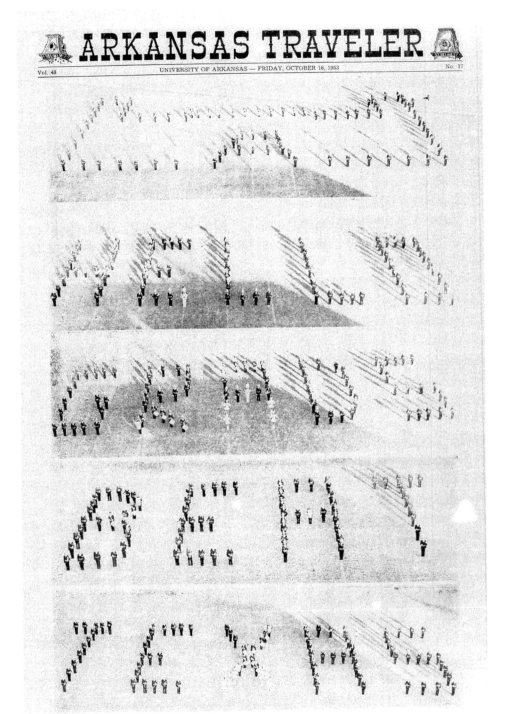

The Arkansas-Texas game of 1953 brought with it the usual excitement of years previous and since. The Razorback Band joined in the spirit of the week spelling out "H-E-L-L-O" "G-R-A-D-S" "B-E-A-T" "T-E-X-A-S" for photos that appeared one word per day on the covers of the Monday through Thursday editions of the *Arkansas Traveler*. On Friday all four photos were reprinted together to engulf the front page as shown at right.

As in years past Razorback Band members played at all the 1953–54 home basketball games. Many also played in the Concert Band performing concerts in the Fine Arts Concert Hall as pictured above.

A highlight of the year was the Razorback Band's participation in a trip to New York in July of 1954 representing Arkansas at the International Lion's Club Convention. The photo above shows the band as it marched through the wet New York City streets to the Convention Center.

After the band returned from its trip to New York City in the summer of 1954, E. J. Marty designed some of the fall halftime shows to reflect places the band had visited. The right formation is of the Liberty Bell, which the band saw during the Philadelphia stopover.

THE MARTY-WIDDER YEARS, 1948–1956

For all of the Razorback Band's in-state trips and for its journeys to play TCU in Fort Worth and Georgia Tech in the Cotton Bowl, buses were the mode of travel in 1954–55 as shown at left.

The Razorback Band (right) was part of the send-off committee for the football team's out-of-state SWC ballgames in 1954.

For 1954–55 the band is shown below performing one of its many concerts on campus. Those presentations occurred most often in the Fine Arts Concert Hall, though an occasional performance took place in the Student Union Ballroom.

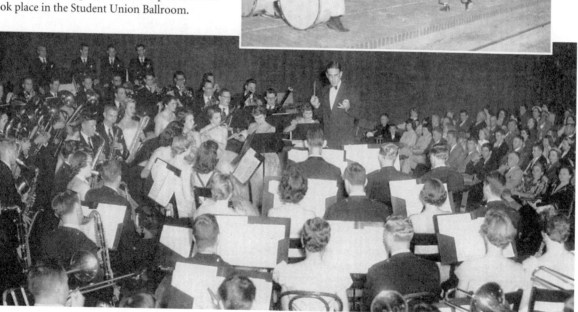

Not only did Bowden Wyatt's Razorbacks go 8-2 for the 1954–55 season, they also beat Texas for the first time since 1948. As a result they won the right to play Georgia Tech in the Cotton Bowl and took the Razorback Band to the game. Though Arkansas lost 14–6, the season turned around the football program. Unfortunately, Wyatt resigned at the end of the season to take on the head coaching job of his alma mater, the University of Tennessee. In the above photo, the Razorback Band forms the familiar "U of A" on the field at the Cotton Bowl game played January 1, 1955.

Part of the duties of Lambda Chapter's Kappa Kappa Psi pledge class in the spring of 1955 was the playing of a concert on the steps of the library during the noon hour as shown at right.

In the picture at right the Razorback Band makes final checks before performing at halftime during the 1955 Cotton Bowl. After that game the band returned to campus to concentrate on playing for basketball games and performing at concert events.

In the fall of 1955, E. J. Marty left his position as director of the Razorback Band after seven very eventful seasons for reasons mentioned in the introduction of this chapter. Roger Widder, Marty's assistant and the woodwind instructor, took over as interim director for the 1955–56 season. From the fall of 1954 until the Cotton Bowl game of 1961, Lewis Epley Jr. (shown left with basketball coach Glen Rose in the press box in 1955) served as the first official Voice of the Razorback Band. A clarinet player in high school, he lost the use of his right hand during a bout with polio, but over the years became a fixture of the Razorback Band with his announcing.

The Razorback Band marched at the usual Little Rock and Fayetteville games in 1955 in addition to traveling to Dallas where Arkansas defeated SMU during the regularly scheduled SWC game played in the Cotton Bowl Stadium.

Head majorette Gail Wood was a very popular twirling captain and eventually was crowned Miss U of A and named runner-up to the National Football Queen.

The above photo shows the Razorback Band in 1955 entering the field for a halftime show in War Memorial Stadium led by drum major Bob Griffin.

During pregame ceremonies at the 1955 TCU-Arkansas game played in Fayetteville, both schools' bands combined forces to play each other's alma maters as shown above.

Though the Arkansas football team went 5-4-1 for the 1955 season, spirits were high on the Hogs all year long.

A photo from the 1955 U of A Homecoming game shows the Razorback Band in the familiar "Old Main" formation for the crowning of the Homecoming royalty.

Interim director Roger Widder (right) monitors the Razorback Band as the group plays for a downtown pep rally in Dallas prior to the SMU tilt of 1955.

After the SMU game (which Arkansas won 6–0), the Razorback Band took to the field in a victory march. A band tradition at the time included wearing caps backwards during the victory march after the game as shown above.

The Concert Band presented a series of concerts in the Fine Arts Concert Hall on campus during the spring of 1956. One featured the world famous trumpeter, Raphael Mendez (pictured at right).

The University of Arkansas
PRESENTS THE

CONCERT BAND

1956 Tour

ROGER WIDDER, Director

In 1956, Widder also took the Concert Band on tour across north Arkansas playing concerts at twelve high schools to showcase the band's talent as well as recruit future members. Shown above is a photo of the band's herald trumpets that graced the cover of the tour's program.

When Richard Worthington began his tenure as director of bands for the University of Arkansas, he brought with him a lot of experience regarding marching and concert bands. A graduate of the University of Michigan and nationally known for leading the Hobart High School Band (Indiana) to five consecutive national awards for excellence, his most recent directing position had been at Vander Cook College of Music in Chicago. At the time of his interview for the U of A, he was finishing his doctorate at the University of Illinois. He stated that it was his intent to continue the "many fine traditions of the Razorback Band, among them the awards system and the fast Michigan State style marching [that] Marty's musicians [had] made popular throughout the state and the South." In addition he had experience in the development of a series of instructional marching films produced at the University of Indiana.

Worthington met with quite a bit of expectation and enthusiasm from the U of A band students since he had promised that the marching style would continue in the manner of the fast high-stepping pace to which they were accustomed. Eighty-one students made up the band that fall, slightly up from the previous year but short of the strength of the Marching 100 of before. In an attempt to give the band a more distinctive moniker and to allow for growth to more than one hundred members in future years, Worthington dubbed the band the Marching Razorbacks, which has remained the band's calling card for almost fifty years. Indeed, by the time he left the university in 1970, the band had grown to more than 150 members.

Longevity apparently was the order of the day at the time. During Worthington's fourteen years on the campus, he worked with only two head football coaches (two years with Jack Mitchell and twelve with Frank Broyles) and two basketball coaches (ten seasons with Glen Rose and four with Duddy Waller).

During Worthington's watch the Razorback Band witnessed and became beneficiaries to the great national and conference successes of the Hogs' football squad. Under Broyles's leadership, the team developed into a winning powerhouse on the field and were consistently seen as contenders for the SWC crown and regular invitees to major post-season bowl games. And with the increasing exposure of the team on regional and national television, the band was introduced

CHAPTER 8

The Worthington Years

1956–1970

to an ever-widening audience of viewers. Success on the field also led to the expansion of Razorback Stadium and full-house audiences there and in Little Rock's War Memorial Stadium. All of that only added to the pressures on Worthington and the Razorback Band to perform new and innovative halftime shows on the field and play spirited and supportive music from the stands. When the Hogs won the national championship in 1964–65 during a twenty-two game winning streak, the Marching Razorbacks experienced a national exposure unparalleled in its existence, and in this author's eyes, stood up to the test.

During Worthington's tenure the band's first black member, Geneva Hill, an alto saxophone player, joined the group in 1964. She was joined the following year by the first black male student, a tenor sax player named James Seawood.

Probably the most controversial subject during Worthington's time at the University of Arkansas was the desire by some campus groups to remove "Dixie" from the band's repertoire at athletic and campus events. Strong feelings on both sides of the issue arose during the last few years that Worthington served as the school's band director and especially when he eventually decided in the fall of 1969 not to play the tune anymore. Courageous an act that it was, he and the band felt the effects for a long time afterward. In fact, his successor would have to deal with the fallout for years to come.

Over the years Doc Worthington and his various assistant directors took the Marching Razorbacks to new heights in the slipstream of the football team and raised the Concert Band to a new level of performance in its singular presentations. And he left behind such a legacy of goodwill among band members and the faculty that he was frequently invited back for special celebrations and anniversaries to be honored for his many contributions to the organization.

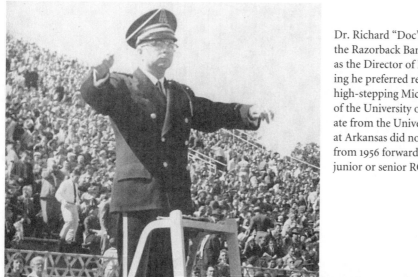

Dr. Richard "Doc" Worthington took over the baton of the Razorback Bands in the summer of 1956 and served as the Director of Bands until 1970. The style of marching he preferred reflected that of the very successful high-stepping Michigan State Band. He was a graduate of the University of Michigan and received his doctorate from the University of Illinois. Worthington's duties at Arkansas did not include directing the ROTC Band; from 1956 forward the ROTC Band was conducted by a junior or senior ROTC student.

In 1956 the Razorback Band made its single out-of-state football trip to the TCU game in Fort Worth via Scotchlite-decorated charter buses as shown at right. The TCU halftime show centered around a three-ring circus theme. TCU defeated the Hogs before a national audience 41–6.

One of the 1956 Razorback Band half-time shows featured a formation of a football player kicking a football down the field while the band played "Mr. Touchdown" in honor of the Arkansas football coach, Jack Mitchell.

In Little Rock for the 1956 Ole Miss game, the Razorback Band gathered on the steps of the Arkansas State Capitol for a pep rally after which the Hogs defeated the Rebels, 14–0. In order to accommodate a band expected to be larger than one hundred members, Worthington began referring to the Marching 100 as the Marching Razorback Band.

Although the football team did not go to a post-season game in 1956, they did have a winning season of 6-4. A season of exciting games and invigorating pep rallies kept the Razorback Band enthusiastic about the year. The photo at right shows the drum line at a pep rally in the Greek Theatre.

In the spring of 1957 "Doc" Worthington and his assistant director, Lloyd Schmidt, led the Concert Band in three on-campus concerts, one of which featured Dona Field, Betty Kelly, and Jerry Gusewell playing with the band on "Bugler's Holiday." Dona and Betty are shown left in rehearsal for the number with Doc. Also in a return engagement Raphael Mendez was a guest soloist for the second concert.

Head majorette Mary Vee Kennedy was the U of A band's featured twirler during the 1957 season. Though the tension was very present in Little Rock due to President Eisenhower's having called out the National Guard to insure a safe integration of Central High School, the Razorback Band still traveled to all three games played that year in the city. They also bused it to the Ole Miss game played in Memphis, and smaller pep bands accompanied the team to other away games played in Texas.

Preston and Kathryn Woodruff, the owners of Vickers Laundry and Cleaners (later renamed Woodruff's Cleaners) served as gracious and enthusiastic chaperones for the Razorback Band's road trips from 1954 to well into the 1980s. To salute their service to the band, the school's Kappa Kappa Psi and Tau Beta Sigma chapters dedicated the 1958 program of the District VI Convention held at the University of Arkansas to them. The photo at right was printed in that program.

The above photos of Kappa Kappa Psi and Tau Beta Sigma band members were printed in the program of the 1958 District VI Convention that was held on the campus of the University of Arkansas.

After three seasons of less than stellar win-loss records, Jack Mitchell resigned as head coach of the Razorback football team and was promptly replaced with Frank Broyles who would coach at the school for the next nineteen seasons. The basketball team tied for first place in the SWC under Coach Glen Rose in 1958.

Doc Worthington directed the 1958 Concert Band in a series of well-received concerts that spring, culminating in the April 30 presentation featuring guest conductor Gene Witherspoon, band director at Arkansas Tech and former student director of the U of A Band. The guest performer was Alfred Gallodoro, considered by many to be America's best reed instrumentalist (he formerly played with the Paul Whiteman Orchestra). During the summer of 1958 Worthington held the first Band Camp on campus for the benefit of developing the skills of high-school musicians.

Frank Broyles's tenure as the Hogs' new head coach was heralded as the dawn of a new era at the U of A, but he started the 1958 season with six straight losses before ending on a four-game winning streak. Nevertheless, the Razorback Band led by drum majors George Jernigan (shown at left with Worthington) and Clyde Pope marched throughout the season with a keen sense of mission.

The Razorback Band takes the field in 1958 at Razorback
Stadium. Notice the drum majors beginning their famous
running strut from inside the band's ranks.

In 1958 the entire Razorback Band bused it to Little Rock for three football games and to Fort Worth for their traditional rivalry against TCU. The above bandsmen arrive at the Worth Hotel in Fort Worth anxious for the game to start. TCU won 12–7.

Invasion of the Marion Hotel in Little Rock took place in the afternoon before the 1958 Arkansas–Ole Miss game. Leading the band was a cadence supplied by the drummers.

After the 1958 football team had lost its first six games of the season, Arkansas won the last four contests, and the band was once again able to march its victory snake dance down the field with hats worn rearward.

John Farris (right) enthusiastically beat the Razorback bass drum throughout the 1958 football season. Afterward, band students joined the basketball Pep Band and/or played in the Concert Band under the direction of Worthington and his new assistant, Fred Miller. Miller would later become Dr. Fred Miller, Dean, College of Music, DePaul University.

Assistant Director Fred Miller (left) and Director Dr. Richard Worthington watch a Razorback Band rehearsal in the fall of 1959. Themes for halftime shows that year included "September 26—A Great Day in History," "Music from Television" and "A Salute to the Undefeated U of A Football Team of 1909."

Band Day 1959 at the U of A (above) involved twenty-eight area high-school bands from Arkansas and Oklahoma joining the Razorback Band on the field spelling out "S-O-U-S-A."

Rehearsal sessions in 1959 for the Razorback Band included two-hour afternoon practices four days a week plus drill field touch-ups on Saturdays before a game. The last-minute-rehearsal photo at right was taken prior to the Tulsa game.

Despite drizzle that threatened the Homecoming Parade in 1959, the Razorback Band marched along Dickson Street leading floats and dignitaries to the campus.

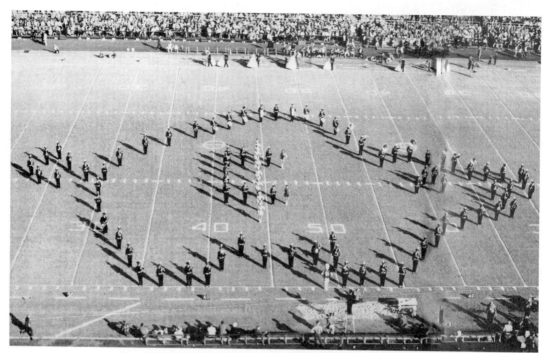

Homecoming 1959 paid special tribute to the fiftieth anniversary of the undefeated season of the 1909 football team. The Razorback Band created formations representing the significant events occurring in 1909 including the beginning of Christmas Savings Banks (note the outline of a piggy bank and the cent sign in the center).

With an 8-2 record for the regular 1959 season, the Razorbacks won a bid to play in the Gator Bowl in Jacksonville, Florida, on New Year's Day 1960. And they won 14–7. In a special issue of the *Traveler* saluting the team members, an ad taken out by the Boston Store included a photo acknowledging the band's excellent majorette line. Besides playing at basketball games during the spring semester, band members played concerts in the Concert Band, participated in the Arkansas Intercollegiate Band, and hosted the Northwest Arkansas Region Festival of the Arkansas School Band and Orchestra Association.

To open the 1960 football season, the Razorback Band acquired a fresher look with new uniforms for the newly expanded 115-member squad. With ten-inch high shako hats and red and white jacket overlays, the outfits sported tuxedo-styled suits beneath, which were used with bowties and white shirts for concert season.

The photo at right shows the Razorback Band on stage of the Greek Theatre during the announcement of the Homecoming royalty for 1960.

An event often held during Homecoming was the Legislative Lunch in the U of A Student Union, where state and campus politicos could evaluate the progress of state funding with regard to the university. In the photo above the Razorback Band entertains diners at the 1960 luncheon.

The Arkansas football team repeated much of their success on the field from the previous year and earned the right to represent the SWC in the 1961 Cotton Bowl (the 1960–61 regular season record of 8-2 included losses to only Baylor and Ole Miss; the Hogs beat Texas 24–23 in Austin). The left photo documents the band's appearance in the Cotton Bowl Parade with featured twirler Kay McCollum and drum major Richard Bush in the foreground. Note the television camera to the left broadcasting the parade live nationwide.

During the 1961 Cotton Bowl game, the Kilgore Rangerettes joined the U of A and Duke Bands in providing the halftime entertainment. In a stirring second half Duke overpowered the Hogs and won the tilt 7–6.

THE WORTHINGTON YEARS, 1956–1970

On its spring calendar, the Concert Band played three concerts on campus in the Fine Arts Concert Hall and two twilight concerts in the Greek Theatre. In addition, the ensemble played for the inauguration ceremony for the new University of Arkansas president, Dr. David Mullins.

The 1962 *Razorback* displayed the photo at left of the students who led the 122-member Razorback Band for 1961–62. The two drum majors were Joe Bob Norwood (far left) and Dick Burton, and Kay McCollum returned as featured twirler once again.

While the 1961 football team continued
its winning ways, the Razorback Band
honed its marching and playing skills
during halftime shows with themes of
"Back to School," "Songs from the
South", and "The Time Show." The
above photo shows various reactions
of band members to a critical play
during a game.

Stadium lights in War Memorial Stadium made
night games possible in Little Rock, whereas the
lack of them made day games necessary when
played in Razorback Stadium in the 1960s. This
would change with time.

With another regular season record of 8-2 in 1961, Arkansas was invited to play Alabama in the January 1, 1962, Sugar Bowl in New Orleans. For the Razorback Band it was an opportunity to once again appear on national television during the Sugar Bowl Parade and at halftime of the game. But sadly the Crimson Tide prevailed at game's end 10–3.

In addition to regular on-campus spring concerts, twilight performances, and basketball gigs in 1962, University of Arkansas audiences were also treated to ensemble concerts by the Brass Choir and the Percussion Ensemble. The latter was conducted by master's candidate Larry McCormick, who later became a vital force in the corps style marching movement, which led to the national school competition known as Bands of America. Also Arthur Fiedler and the Boston Pops Orchestra and Harry James gave special concerts on the Fayetteville campus that year.

To open the 1962–63 football season, the Razorback Band played the alma mater in the ever-familiar U of A formation at the Oklahoma State game in War Memorial Stadium. Forty thousand fans packed the stands in anticipation of another winning Razorback season. The following week twenty-four high-school bands (more than 1,750 musicians) joined the Razorback Band at the Tulsa game for Band Day in Fayetteville.

Following a trip to TCU where the Razorbacks began their 1962 SWC race (Arkansas won 42–14), the band cheered the team on in Razorback Stadium as the Hogs won 28–2 against Baylor on Dad's Day. Shown is featured twirler Kay McCollum.

Prior to the 1962 Homecoming game played against Rice, the Razorback Band (above) marched in the annual parade through the streets and around the town square in Fayetteville. Drum majors Joe Bob Norwood and Sandy Porter led the way.

Homecoming halftime festivities in 1962 reflected traditions of years past with the Razorback Band forming the musical backdrop for the day. Other halftime shows that season featured the band playing a salute to George M. Cohan and a celebration of Latin and Spanish music.

With an incredible 9-1 record (losing only to the Longhorns in Austin) the Razorbacks made a return trip to the Sugar Bowl on January 1, 1963, playing Ole Miss. The Razorback Band also again marched in the Sugar Bowl Parade, making special television appearances (like the one above) and performing at the game. Unfortunately, the team also lost the game again, 17–13.

With the new Science-Engineering Building slated to go up on the site of the Band Building, Worthington and crew moved in January of 1963 to an old World War II surplus building placed north of Gregson Hall. Just over two months later in the early morning hours of March 26, a fire broke out in the Band Building, destroying many instruments, uniforms, records, and a lot of music. Fortunately no one was injured, and the band moved into temporary quarters in the basement of the Fine Arts Building with rehearsals taking place in the Fine Arts Concert Hall. Late in the semester the university announced plans for the construction of a brand-new band building.

The football season for 1963 held much promise after the four previous years culminated in post-season bowl appearances. However, in 1963 the team suffered a humbling 5-5 record. Nevertheless, the 140-member Razorback Band, led by drum majors Sandy Porter and Bill Woolly (left), continued to contribute a much-needed lift in school spirit.

At the pep rallies in 1963 there was a continuing roar against the nature of off-color jokes made by the emcees permeating the events. The majorettes fronting the band at a rally below in the Greek Theatre retained their dignified stance through all of the hubbub. In September of 1963 an Arkansas student, Donna Axum, was crowned Miss America, and Doc Worthington built a halftime show around her for the Texas A & M game that she attended.

On October 3, 1963, the dedication of the newly completed Greer's Ferry Dam and Reservoir at Heber Springs took place with President John F. Kennedy doing the honors. Director Richard Worthington and his new assistant, Ralph Montgomery, had the pleasure of directing the Razorback Band, which played at the festivities. Sadly, the president would be the victim of an assassin's bullets seven weeks later.

Though the football team's record for 1963 did not match up to those of pre-vious years, the band took every opportunity to cel-ebrate a victory as can be seen in the left photo after one of the five wins that year. The only out-of-state game to which the band traveled that season was the SMU tilt in Dallas.

Band Day in 1963 was the largest held to date at the U of A with thirty-six high-school and junior-high-school bands consisting of 2,800 musicians. The above formation was performed during pre-game activities for the Tulsa game.

The 1963 concert season at the University of Arkansas began in the fall with the Concert Band performing in the Fine Arts Concert Hall on December 4. Other performances occurred during the second semester often in counterpoint to the Basketball Band's playing at the games in Barnhill Field House.

The 1964–65 Razorback football season was the diamond in Coach Frank Broyles's crown. The team went undefeated for the regular season and claimed the national championship, defeating Nebraska in the Cotton Bowl. And the Razorback Band was there for the ride providing pep and musical support all season long. Linda Purdy (center front), the band's featured twirler, served in that role for two years.

Doc Worthington was in his eighth season as Director of Bands at the U of A in 1964. His new assistant that year was Dr. Lawrence Meyer (shown in uniform at lower right), and Doug Rye was in his third year serving as the Voice of the Razorback Band. Also that year the band moved into its new facilities built across Garland Avenue from the Fine Arts Complex. Nineteen sixty-four also saw the first black student enrolled in the band—she was Geneva Hill, a saxophone player from Little Rock.

Although the band did not travel to the Texas game to witness the Hogs' 14–13 win over the Longhorns, members did serenade the returning players at the airport in the wee hours along with hundreds of other fans. The lone regular season out-of-state trip for the Razorback Band that year was to Fort Worth for the TCU game. At right the band is caught on film performing a special pep rally in Little Rock at the governor's mansion prior to the Baylor game.

At the Cotton Bowl the Razorback Band performed its "kick-step" drill to the music of "Marching Razorback March" composed by assistant director Dr. Lawrence Meyer (note the Kilgore Rangerettes on the sidelines). In the bottom photo the Arkansas and Nebraska bands were joined by five high-school bands traditionally invited to perform a special show at pre-game. The "1-9-6-5" formation signaled the beginning of the new year and Eldon Janzen, later to become Director of Bands at Arkansas, was the guest conductor leading the massed bands in "Auld Lang Syne."

On Friday, February 5, 1965, the Grantland Rice Award was presented to the Razorback football team in a special ceremony in Razorback Stadium. Even though the day was cold, windy, and cloudy, the band exhibited their support and appreciation by playing for the Champions' Day event. The following week, plans were announced for the expansion of Razorback Stadium to 33,204 permanent seats and enough folding-chair and end-zone space to accommodate 40,000 fans.

The Concert Band's 1965 season concluded with a presentation in the Student Union Ballroom featuring Doc Severinsen of *The Tonight Show* fame as guest trumpet soloist (note the program at right).

UNIVERSITY OF ARKANSAS
DEPARTMENT OF MUSIC

The University of Arkansas Concert Band

RICHARD A. WORTHINGTON, *Conductor*
LAURENCE J. MEYER, *Associate Conductor*
CARL "DOC" SEVERINSEN, *Trumpet Soloist*

Student Union   Sunday, 3:00 P.M.

Ballroom   May 16, 1965

Sea Songs, Quick March	R. Vaughan Williams
Siegfried's Rhine Journey from "Gotterdammerung"	Richard Wagner
Somersault	Hale Smith
L'Idoita, Passo Doppio Sinfonico	John Jannotta
Reflections Past	W. Francis McBeth
West Point Symphony	Robert J. Dvorak

Finale — Allegro Spiritoso

INTERMISSION

The Improvisator, Overture	Eugen D'Albert
Dialogue for Trumpet and Band	John Krance
The Painted Desert	Walter Levinsky
Soliloquy for Trumpet	John J. Morrissey

Soloist — Carl "Doc" Severinsen

Pictures At An Exhibition   M. Moussorgsky

The Hut of Baba-Yaga
The Great Gate of Kiev

For the 1965–66 marching season Sandy Porter (standing) and Bill Woolly led the band for the third consecutive year as a team. The bottom photo presents the ten-woman majorette line for that season flanked by a new pair of featured twirlers, Johnny Helms and Judy Dupree. The band's announcer in the press box was Phil Byrd.

Below: For the 1965 Texas-Arkansas game played in Razorback Stadium, Doc Severinsen returned to the campus as the Razorback Band's guest soloist during its halftime show. During the season, the Marching Razorbacks appeared on national television twice and on regional television once.

From the National Champion success of the previous season, great expectations were present for the Razorbacks to repeat in 1965–66 with a carryover of many of the team's players. Also present was the essence of "bigness" in terms of national recognition and besting everything big that was in Texas. The University of Texas band had always touted their large playable eight-foot-diameter bass drum (dubbed Big Bertha) as being the nation's largest. For 1965, Marty Rosen of the Rosen Music Company in Little Rock built a new ten-foot-three-inch drum named Big Red (shown above) for the Arkansas Band to exhibit during games. Despite the fact that the drum could not be played due to the fragility of its heads, it made quite a visual impact at games, which can be seen in subsequent photos.

Drum majors Porter and Woolly set a high standard for strutting when the Marching Razorbacks took to the field during pre-game and halftime entrances. The marching unit, numbering about 140 members, marched at all in-state games and at the SMU game played in Dallas. It also sent a pep band to all other out-of-state games.

By the end of the regular football season in 1965, the Razorbacks had once again gone 10-0 and amassed a 22-0 winning streak culminating with the defeat of Texas Tech on November 20. The Arkansas and Texas Tech Bands (shown left) performed a combined pre-game show before the contest, playing each another's alma maters and the national anthem.

With its perfect regular-season record the Razorbacks returned to the Cotton Bowl on January 1, 1966, to defend its national title, but lost to LSU by a score of 14–7. Prior to the game the massed bands that had marched in the Cotton Bowl Parade joined the Arkansas and LSU bands for the televised spectacular shown left.

The 1966 concert season at the U of A included concerts played on the university campus and separate tours for the Concert Band (to eight Arkansas high schools across the state, March 30–April 1) and for the Brass Choir (for audiences in Arkansas, Oklahoma, and New Mexico, February 13–25). Shown above is the Brass Choir conducted by Lawrence Meyer (at right).

In the fall of 1966, Dr. Richard Worthington welcomed a new assistant director and woodwind instructor into the fold—David Pittman. Lawrence Meyer remained as the brass instructor and arranged music for the halftime shows. Bill Woolly and John Richardson served as drum majors for the 150-member band, and Julie Ellis and Rick Lowery (shown) were named as the new featured twirlers.

After two big seasons as beneficiaries of the football team's success and notoriety, Worthington and company planned big halftime shows that created a lot of excitement. Shows built around "Show Hits" and "The Music of Henry Mancini" stirred the crowds as the Razorbacks went on to another winning season. Left the 1966 Razorback Band takes a bow at the end of a performance.

Once again in 1966, the band marched at all of the Fayetteville games and two of the Little Rock games, and traveled by bus to the Texas game played in Austin (where Arkansas won its third consecutive game against the Longhorns 12–7). The above photo shows the majorettes encouraging the team from the stands.

In 1966 the Razorbacks tallied an 8-2 record, but that was not good enough to be invited to a major bowl in post season. Broyles opted not to take the team to a minor bowl that year, so the Marching Razorbacks saw no bowl-game exposure for only the second time in the previous eight seasons.

Glen Rose, who had been a U of A basketball fixture for many years (he had coached the cagers from 1933 to 1942 and again from 1952 to 1966), yielded his position to a new man in 1966—Duddy Waller. The photo at right shows the Razorback Basketball Pep Band (conducted by assistant director David Pittman) playing at a game in Barnhill Field House.

Doc Worthington and David Pittman led the Concert Band in a series of concerts in the spring of 1967 culminating in a performance in the Fine Arts Concert Hall featuring Prelude to Act I of *La Traviata* by Verdi and Symphony in F Minor no. 4 by Tchaikovsky.

In 1967 after three high-profile winning seasons, the Razorback football team saw its first losing season since Broyles's inaugural year in 1958. In spite of it all, the Marching Razorbacks promoted school spirit when they marched in the Homecoming Parade prior to the Texas A& M game.

The only out-of-state game traveled to by the entire Razorback Band in 1967 was the Baylor game played in Waco. At right can be seen the smaller Pep Band which made it to Houston and cheered the Razorbacks to victory against the Rice Owls 23–9.

Leading the band onto the field in 1967 were drum majors John Richardson and Gary Ricketts (shown in center of the right photo). Barnhill Field House, the site of home basketball games, can be seen in the background. The Marching Razorbacks' halftime shows that year were built around the music of George M. Cohan, popular marches, and famous motion picture themes. Alan Epley was the band's announcer.

When Texas arrived in Little Rock's War Memorial Stadium for the continuation of the Razorback-Longhorn rivalry, both schools' bands combined on the field for pre-game performances of their alma maters and the national anthem. Texas broke Arkansas's three-year hold over the Longhorns that day winning 21–12.

The left photo shows band members posing in front of the Razorback Band Building that was completed in 1964. Originally built to accommodate about 150 members, the structure would burst at its seams later as the organization grew.

In the summer of 1967 trophies for Outstanding Chapters in the USA for Tau Beta Sigma and Kappa Kappa Psi were won by the U of A's Psi and Lambda Chapters respectively, the first time one school's chapters were so honored simultaneously. In subsequent years, Lambda Chapter would win the award on two more occasions.

The U of A concert season for 1967–68 featured the Brass Choir on tour in December to high-school audiences in Central Arkansas and the Concert Band on tour in March to a different set of high-school audiences also in Central Arkansas. The photos above were printed on the program of the Brass Choir's tour. Performers included Randy Lee (voice and announcer); Jeff Emory, Dean Papp, Eddie Hardister, Dale Forbes, Allen Wight, Truitt Gray (trumpets); Joe Cross, Gary Ricketts, Cheryl Crites (French horn); Connie Wing (percussion); Joe Pelphrey, Larry Kinder, Joe Jones (trombones); Larry Ricketts (baritone); and Lawrence Beck (tuba). Dr. Lawrence J. Meyer conducted.

Nineteen sixty-eight saw a tremendous turnaround in the Arkansas football arena. The Razorbacks returned to their winning ways and even capitalized on a post-season bowl game. Left, Razorback Band members charge down the steps of the Greek Theatre at the beginning of yet another boisterous and often off-color pep rally.

Halftime shows for the Marching Razorbacks' 1968 season (once again announced by Alan Epley) centered around the themes of "Talking Up Arkansas" and "Something Old, Something Featured, Something New." In addition to appearing at all the home games and traveling to the TCU game in Fort Worth, the band also played at the dedication of the Terry Lock and Dam on the Arkansas River and at Derby Day at Hot Springs' Oaklawn Park.

The 1968 Razorback Band is shown marching into the home stadium ready for another exciting ballgame and well-rehearsed halftime show. Leading the band were drum majors John Richardson and Gary Ricketts followed by featured twirlers Betsy Burroughs, Rick Lowery, and Julie Ellis. One issue that gained momentum during the year was the objection to the playing of "Dixie" at ballgames and pep rallies. It remained a staple of the band's repertoire for the time being.

Finishing the regular 1968 season with a 9-1 record (the only loss coming against Texas) the Hogs received the coveted invitation to play in the Sugar Bowl in New Orleans on New Year's Day 1969. Playing the favored Georgia Bulldogs, the Razorbacks won 16–2. At halftime (shown left) the Marching Razorbacks put on a show marching to "Waiting for the Robert E. Lee," "March of the Young Romans," and "Joshua." The band left the field to the strains of "Dixie."

During the spring semester of 1968 the debate continued in the student press and across the campus with no resolution about the appropriateness of the playing of "Dixie" at campus events. Also, SWC basketball continued to be played in Barnhill with the Pep Band in attendance, and the Concert Band presented a special performance in the Fine Arts Concert Hall featuring internationally acclaimed saxophonist Sigurd Rascher.

The school year 1969–70 was Richard "Doc" Worthington's fourteenth and last as Director of Bands. He subsequently accepted a position as chair of the Music Department at Northeast Louisiana State College.

In the fall of 1969, led by drum majors Gary Ricketts and Tommy Thompson and featured twirlers Betsy Burroughs and Melody Schwalm, the band headed for another pep rally in the Greek Theatre on the U of A campus.

Hanging over the entire 1969–70 football season and extending on again into the spring was the "Dixie" issue. After a series of student-senate votes, a campus-wide referendum, and numerous confrontations of which a few turned violent, Dr. Worthington discontinued the band's playing of the song just prior to the Texas-Arkansas Great Shootout of 1969. Shown right are band members facing a polarized group of students during a pep rally.

The 1969 Razorback Band prepares to march down the field for pre-game ceremonies. Once again the football team came up with a winning formula to post a 9-1 season losing only to Texas in what was famously billed as the "Great Shootout" between number one ranked Texas and number two ranked Arkansas. President Nixon even attended the game.

After a controversial 15–14 loss to Texas in the Great Shootout the Razorbacks received a second consecutive bid to play in the Sugar Bowl against Ole Miss on January 1, 1970. Shown above at halftime of the game, the Marching Razorbacks dressed in new red and white uniforms presented a show entitled, "Arkansas, Land of Opportunity."

On May 3, 1970, Dr. Richard "Doc" Worthington conducted his final concert with the University of Arkansas Concert Band, featuring the music of *Die Meistersinger* by Wagner-Hindsley and *Slavonic Rhapsody* by Friedemann-Lake. David Pittman also made his final appearance during the concert. (He became the band director at Bryan Adams High School in Dallas.)

In February of 1970, it was announced that Eldon Janzen of Irving, Texas, had been appointed Director of Bands at the University. At the time Janzen was Director of Music Activities for the Irving Public School System. A native Oklahoman, he served two years in the U. S. Ordnance Corps and completed his master's studies in conducting at North Texas University. He subsequently developed superior performing bands in New Boston and Greenville before moving to Irving in 1962. He had developed a strong reputation as educator, conductor, and adjudicator throughout the Southwest. Early in the summer of 1970, Janzen took over as the new Director of Bands at the University of Arkansas, conducting the Marching Razorbacks and the Symphonic and Varsity Bands.

In keeping with having students report to rehearsal a week before school started, Janzen began practice sessions on August 31. Whereas the upperclassmen had been accustomed to the high-stepping fast-paced Michigan State–style maneuvers, Janzen subscribed to the more subdued military marching movements that he had had much success with in Texas. Though there was some resistance from "that's-not-the-way-we-used-to-do-it" veteran members, Janzen persevered in convincing the band to "do it his way." His ultimate goal was to stress the importance of good quality ensemble sound while performing marching maneuvers.

Eldon Janzen also released a statement regarding the playing of "Dixie" which included the following:

> It is my feeling that to resume the use of this song after its termination by the previous Band Director could produce detrimental effects to the reputation of the University, running also a decided risk of conflict on the University campus which could bring about bodily harm to students under my supervision. . . .
>
> Further, I feel that the University Band should not be cast in the role of formulating either political or administrative policy by once again becoming embroiled in this matter. Our job is to conduct such musical activities as would complement this school and promote school spirit which would serve to unite our student body and our supporters. I interpreted the playing of "Dixie" to be a tool of dissent at this juncture. . . .
>
> Finally I must say that I am reluctant to become involved in this issue because of the responsibility I feel that I owe to the

CHAPTER 9

The Janzen Years

1970–1985

parents of each of the men and women who take part in the University Band under my direction. These students contribute far more of their time and efforts than the credit value of any similar course requires. I think the possibility of injury and violence over this issue is real. I would prefer not to expose them to such a possibility on the basis of my decision to play this song.

Throughout the fall, letters were sent to Janzen, pro and con, regarding his decision not to play the song, and articles popped up in newspapers across the state in addition to taking up an inordinate amount of space in the campus *Traveler*. But Janzen held his ground and the song went unplayed.

It is probably safe to say that the marching style and sound of the Razorback Band changed more under his tutelage than any other director's before him or since. As previously mentioned, he supplanted the previous high-stepping cadence of his predecessor with a more subdued military gait that over the years gave way to a peppier and more up-tempo snap until it evolved into a style that was more drum-and-bugle-corps brassy in sound and angular and abstract in the formations that appeared on the field. He incorporated the now famous "Big A" formation during pre-game ceremonies and instituted the standard by which the band to this day finishes its halftime performances. Though it began with the simple spell-out of "A-R-K" morphing into "H-O-G," a bit of tweaking over the years and the addition of more band members led eventually to the "G-O H-O-G-S" formation and the announcer's impassioned question "What's that spell?" And he also added the tag line "The Best in Sight and Sound" to the band's introductions to the crowds.

Growing to as many as 220 members meant that taking the band to Little Rock and out-of-state games became more expensive, and the uniform inventory often was stretched past its limits. There were years when the band was seen on the field in three different uniforms in order to get everyone outfitted. And then when the budget was at its tightest, Janzen opted to clad the whole band in informal red poplin jackets and white trousers rather than have band members wearing remnants of tattered old uniforms.

Eldon Janzen also took a lot of flack from the powers that be and not just a few influential alumni when a black student, Sanford Tollette, was chosen to be a drum major in 1971. And he stood up to the plate and accepted the position of interim chair of the Music Department in 1981–82 when a search committee could not agree on whom to hire for that position. In addition, he could be quite vocal when discussing with the university administration the need for larger facilities to accommodate the growing band program or the subject of off-color jokes and blue humor during pep rallies in the Greek Theatre. He was even brought into the fray when directors of some SWC bands refused to bring their bands to Arkansas because of abuse their band members had undergone at the hands and mouths of unruly Razorback fans. But through it all, Eldon Janzen held his head high and pressed forward for excellence from the Marching Razorbacks in performance and presentation.

The Razorback Band did manage to attend a number of bowl games because of the success of the Hogs' and saw their share of basketball games won in Barnhill Field House after Eddie Sutton came on board as coach. But Janzen's sense of pride seemed to spill over when the Wind Ensemble, Wind Symphony, or Concert Band performed exceptionally well during a concert on campus or on tour.

In 1984, Eldon Janzen yielded the responsibilities of the Marching Razorbacks to Chalon Ragsdale but retained the title and responsibilities of Director of Bands until 1995. Today he holds the position of Director of Bands, Emeritus and often visits the band building that has its main rehearsal hall named in his honor.

Eldon Janzen, a graduate of North Texas State University and more recently supervisor of the Irving (Texas) High School music program, took the reins as Director of Bands at the University of Arkansas in the fall of 1970. When he stood by the decision of his predecessor not to reintroduce "Dixie" to games and pep rallies, he took a lot of flak but held firm. Janzen chose Robert Umiker to fill the position of assistant director and woodwind specialist. Gerald Sloan was named as the low brass instructor and Robert Bright continued in his role as principal brass instructor and director of the Brass Choir, having come on board the previous spring.

The first football game of the 1970 season was played against Stanford University in Little Rock's War Memorial Stadium. With Chevrolet as the NCAA television sponsor, the car company and ABC-TV held a year-long All-American Band Contest among the schools they were airing that season. The Marching Razorbacks' traditional marching style at the half went up against the Stanford band's unorthodox and ultra-contemporary show with the latter taking the prize. The below photo was taken two weeks later at the Tulsa game played in Fayetteville.

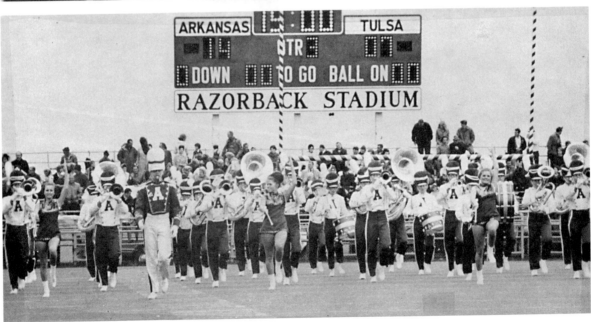

The right photo shows the Marching Razorbacks on the practice field in the fall of 1970. As a fundraising project to raise scholarship funds for the Razorback Band and money for equipment for the Springdale High School Band, the two bands combined their efforts at a Band Rally in the Bulldog Stadium in Springdale.

This 1970 photo catches the Marching Razorbacks during the playing of the Arkansas alma mater prior to a game played in War Memorial Stadium. A closer look at the evenness of the grass on the field reveals the fact that the surface is Astroturf, which was also installed in Razorback Stadium in Fayetteville.

By December 5, 1970, Arkansas's record was 9-1 (only having lost to Stanford) and Texas was 10-0 and ranked number 1 in the country thus setting up "Shootout No. 2" in Austin. The Marching Razorbacks went along for the contest and are shown at left playing a pep rally in Austin prior to the game. Unfortunately the score was heavily tilted in Texas's favor, 42–7. By the time that the game was played, all bowl bids had been extended, so only the winner of the Texas-Arkansas match-up saw action on New Year's Day.

In November 1970, Dale Bumpers was elected governor of Arkansas, and he invited the Razorback Band to march in his inaugural parade in January (as shown right). Bumpers was drum major of the band in 1943.

After a number of spring concerts for the Wind Ensemble (the university's audition band) and the Brass Choir, the 1971 season wrapped up with a concert played in the Fine Arts Concert Hall on May 2 featuring Francis McBeth as guest conductor. Director Eldon Janzen is pictured above with the Wind Ensemble.

In 1970 Frank Broyles asked Director Eldon Janzen if he could devise a slick band formation through which the football team could run onto the field. After a few ill-fated attempts at the end of the 1970 season (see photo above), Janzen devised a new formation over the summer of 1971. The right photo shows the result of his efforts, which remains a tradition into the twenty-first century.

Also added as a new feature to the Razorback Band in 1971 was a flag line which still graces the band's appearances. The band (172 members) was growing in size faster than its new uniform inventory; thus the flag members and percussionists wore the old-style uniforms.

A third milestone of the 1971 Marching Razorbacks was the selection of the first African American as drum major. He was Sanford Tollette shown at right with twirlers Jan Wallace, Debbie Cox, Kathy Hunsacker, Nancy Meyer, Kathy Rice, Beba Kirkham, and head drum major Dwight Estes.

THE JANZEN YEARS, 1970–1985

Halftime shows for 1971 centered around a number of themes including a country-western show featuring guest star Leon McAuliffe (right), who joined the band in playing his "Steel Guitar Rag." Other shows included an "Armed Forces Salute," "A Classical Music Tribute" and the "Celebration of the 100th Anniversary of the U of A."

McAuliffe was a long-time member of the famous Bob Wills Texas Playboys and made his home in Rogers, Arkansas, as owner of a local radio station until his death.

The band's only out-of-state trip in 1971 was to Dallas for the SMU tilt, but a pep band from the group made it to the other SWC contests because of the efforts of the band's Kappa Kappa Psi (left) and Tau Beta Sigma chapter members. A year when Arkansas beat USC and Texas, lost to Tulsa and Texas A & M and tied with Rice left the Hogs with an 8-2-1 record and an invitation to play in the Liberty Bowl in Memphis, played on December 20. The Marching Razorbacks performed a Christmas show at the half before the Hogs lost to the Tennessee Vols 14–13. The bowl trip also represented a milestone in the history of the band. Since the game fell during the week of final examinations, air transportation was arranged to shuttle the band to and from Memphis to keep from interrupting the exam schedule. Those students with exams scheduled the morning following the game were flown home first; the rest waited until the second flight and arrived in Fayetteville about sunrise.

One of the highlights of the spring 1972 season was the guest solo performance of Dr. Neill Humfeld (pictured at left) at the February 27 concert of the Symphonic Band conducted by Eldon Janzen. Humfeld was the chair of the Instrumental Music Division at East Texas State University.

The 1972–73 Arkansas football team ended up with a 6-5 record, which earned no post-season bowl bid, but the Marching Razorbacks gave it their all during the fall with halftime shows marched to themes including "Big Band Music of the '40s," "TV Show and Commercial Tunes," and a big Halloween show. Director Eldon Janzen is shown below in center front flanked by kneeling drum majors Bill Irwin and Sanford Tollette.

The right two photos were printed in the 1973 *Razorback,* documenting band members marching downfield in a drill routine and Director Eldon Janzen observing the band's movements from the sidelines.

In the early 1970s Eldon Janzen began yet another tradition by having the Marching Razorback Band spell out "A-R-K" and "H-O-G" as its final formation of halftime shows to welcome the football team back onto the field for the second half of play. Over the years the formation would evolve into "G-O H-O-G-S" with the band's announcer inquiring of the crowd "What's that spell?" leading into the "Fight Song" and the band's exit from the field.

The 1972–73 Razorback basketball team under coach Lanny Van Eman went 16-10 on the year for its first winning season since 1965–66 and its best showing since 1960–61.

A highlight of the spring concert season was the premier of Robert Jager's *Overture: Memory of a Friend* commissioned by the Kappa Kappa Psi and Tau Beta Sigma organizations at the university. The piece was dedicated to the memory of Rick Wilkerson of Bentonville who was killed in a tragic automobile accident. Mr. Jager, on staff at Tennessee Tech University, was present in the Fine Arts Concert Hall on May 4 to conduct the Symphonic Band's playing of his composition.

Before the 1973–74 marching season began, Janzen received notices from three fellow SWC band directors that they would not bring their bands to games played in Arkansas because they were "fed up with abuse from Arkansas fans" (the alleged abuse included verbal insults, the throwing of objects, and physical attacks). It was speculated that a second reason for the bands' not traveling to Arkansas was the increasing cost in sending their three-hundred-member bands that far to play. However, Texas A & M did send their band to their game played in Fayetteville and as their director noted, were "well received." The Arkansas Band is shown left marching in a diamond pattern.

Rather than wear a variety of different uniforms because of the increased size of the band (and the state of disrepair of the old uniforms), the Marching Razorbacks were outfitted in white turtleneck shirts and trousers with red poplin jackets for 1973. The band members are shown above marching at the TCU game played in Little Rock.

The formation above by the Marching Razorbacks was performed at Homecoming 1973 (note the convertibles at the bottom of the photo carrying the Homecoming royalty to the field). The band's lone drum major that season was Ken McIntosh, and Luther Meier was the band's new assistant director and announcer. Halftime themes centered around "A Salute to Our Famous Ladies," "Headline Highlights," and "The Spirit of America." The team's schedule ended with a 5-5-1 record precluding a bowl appearance.

The 1974 spring concert season highlights included a biennial tour to north Arkansas high schools by the Symphonic Band and Gerald Sloan's U of A Jazz Band, concluding with concerts on campus April 8 and 9. Also of note was a special celebration in the Student Union Ballroom on April 27, commemorating the one hundredth anniversary of the University of Arkansas Band and the fiftieth anniversary of Lambda Chapter of Kappa Kappa Psi. Former director Dr. Richard Worthington was the guest speaker.

RAZORBACK BAND

Annual Awards Banquet

COMMEMORATING

**The 100th ANNIVERSARY of
The UNIVERSITY BAND**

and

**The 50th ANNIVERSARY of LAMBDA CHAPTER
KAPPA KAPPA PSI**

ARKANSAS UNION BALLROOM
APRIL 27, 1974

The 1974–75 marching season for the Razorback Band began with "early week" as it had in seasons past. This involved the new freshmen arriving at school before the rest of the student body to learn the basics of university marching and playing and then combining with the upperclassmen to polish a show for the first game of the season. The left silhouette and the bottom photo show the band members at work.

Once again in 1974 the Marching Razorbacks took to the field in white slacks and red poplin jackets with drum majors Ken McIntosh and Grady Core out front joined by featured twirlers Barbara Gilley and Jim Fisher.

The two photos on this page show the Razorback Band in action at halftime during 1974 games played in Fayetteville. Themes for the band's shows that season ranged from "Midnight Special" and "March Review," to "Great Days in the Life of Every American."

The entire band traveled to the 1974 Texas game played in Austin, whereas other out-of-town games were attended by the Pep Band. The Hogs ended their season 6-4-1, lacking a bowl bid, but the Razorback basketball team under the leadership of the new coach Eddie Sutton placed second in the SWC and posted a 17-9 record overall.

Eldon Janzen wanted new uniforms for the Marching Razorbacks and found assistance in fundraising efforts with members of Kappa Kappa Psi and Tau Beta Sigma among others in 1974.

738 Organizations

In the fall of 1975, new uniforms arrived just in time to be worn at the first game of the season against Air Force in Little Rock. The uniforms also included a red bolero marching shirt for hot-weather games. One hundred and fifty-seven members marched on the field that year including drum majors Grady Core and Joel Clark and featured twirler Jim Fisher.

The 1975–76 football season turned out to be the best one for the Hogs since 1968–69, even though they lost to Texas and Oklahoma State. Pep rallies on campus were more boisterous than in years past, and by season's end the team ended up in the Cotton Bowl for the first time in ten years. The Marching Razorback majorettes are shown performing at a rally in the Greek Theatre.

The Marching Razorbacks enter the field from the sidelines in preparation for another halftime show in the fall of 1975. Chal Ragsdale joined the band's staff as assistant director that season.

In the above photo the Marching Razorbacks make their appearance in the 1976 Cotton Bowl Parade. And later that afternoon the team defeated the Georgia Bulldogs 31–10 on national television. The Razorback Band marched a show at the half to the music of *The New World Symphony, The Wiz*, and "Don't Rain on My Parade."

The University of Arkansas

at Fayetteville

🔔 presents 🔔

THE BRASS CHOIR

Robert Bright, Conductor

Wednesday, March 10, 1976, 2:10 PM

representing NACWAPI

✿ ✿ ✿ ✿ ✿ and ✿ ✿ ✿ ✿ ✿

THE SYMPHONIC WIND ENSEMBLE

Eldon Janzen, Conductor

Friday, March 12, 1976, 10:30 AM

representing CBDNA

🔔 at the 🔔

National Bicentennial Convention

of

Music Educators National Conference

In March of 1976 the Brass Choir conducted by Robert Bright and the Symphonic Wind Ensemble led by Eldon Janzen performed special concerts at the National Bicentennial Convention of the Music Educators Conference in Atlantic City, New Jersey.

In the fall of 1976, 194 members of the Razorback Band massed for the largest contingent the school had ever had. With a marching unit of 184 the group traveled to all the Little Rock games by bus as well as to the Texas game played in Austin.

THE JANZEN YEARS, 1970–1985

Fronting the Razorback Band for 1976 were drum majors Joel Clark and Grady Core and featured twirler Jim Fisher (center).

Band Day 1976 was held at the Tulsa game with ten area high-school bands joining the Marching Razorbacks for pre-game ceremonies.

Though the 1976 Razorback football team faltered a bit and had a 5-5-1 record, the Razorback Band entered the stadium with expectations of a victory at every game.

The above photo illustrates the 1976 Razorback Band's on-field appearance when the warm-weather red bolero shirts were worn instead of the heavier long-tailed jackets. Halftime shows that season featured the music of George Gershwin, themes from current television programs, and the theme of the Twentieth Olympiad.

Notable for the Symphonic Band in 1977 was its participation on campus with the Brass Choir, Jazz Band, Percussion Ensemble, the Concert Choir, and Schola Cantorum in a Festival Concert performed in the Fine Arts Center on April 20.

For the 1977 season the Hogs had a new coach in Lou Holtz, though Frank Broyles remained as athletic director. The Razorback Band grew to 219 members, Joel Clark and Tony Logue served as its drum majors, and Jim Fisher twirled his way through his fifth season. Band members are shown at left preparing for another exciting marching and football season.

The below ten women served as the majorette line for the 1977 Marching Razorbacks with Kelly Cathey (fifth from right) serving as the head majorette. Robert Bright continued in his role as the Voice of the Razorback Band as he would into the 1980s.

As can be seen right, the 1977 Razorback Band formed the huge "A" on the field through which the football team, cheerleaders, and mascot ran onto the field as the announcement of the players was made prior to the beginning of the games.

THE JANZEN YEARS, 1970–1985

The entire Razorback Band bused it to College Station for the Texas A & M game in 1977 (Arkansas won 26–20). But the season's surprise was that Texas and Houston brought their bands to games played in Arkansas for their first appearances since the allegations of abuse from Arkansas fans in the early 1970s.

Arkansas finished its 1977 regular football season with a record of 10-1 (losing only to Texas) and received an invitation to play Oklahoma in the 1978 Orange Bowl in Miami. Even though Holtz suspended three of his key players for team infractions, the Hogs, quarterbacked by Ron Calcagni, upset the Sooners 31–6 in what was arguably one of the most talked-about games that the Razorbacks ever won. The Razorback Band in its halftime show saluted two of America's vocal treasures, Bing Crosby and Elvis Presley.

The 1977–78 U of A basketball season under Coach Eddie Sutton made history for the team. They tied for first place in the SWC and ended up in the Final Four of the NCAA Tournament ending with a record of 32-4.

A bright spot of the 1978 concert season was the Percussion Ensemble's performance at the Music Educator's National Conference in Chicago. Conducted by Chalon Ragsdale, the group included the selections "Forest Rain" by Du Pont and "Sonatina" by Tull on their program.

The "A-R-K H-O-G" formation of previous years evolved into the "G-O H-O-G" spell-out for 1978. Halftime shows that year featured Chuck Mangione's "Land of Make Believe," *Battlestar Gallactica*, "At the Copa," and "I've Got the Music in Me."

The Razorback Band began its 1978 school year by marching in the Fort Smith Great Raft Race Parade, which benefited the city's United Way and Chamber of Commerce. The band's out-of-state football trip that year took them once again to Austin for the Texas-Arkansas game, which the Longhorns won 28–21.

For 1978 as many as 240 students dressed out for the Razorback Band for halftime shows and parades. Tony Logue and Jon Beard were drum majors for the year and Karen Mosshart was the new featured twirler. Above is pictured the entire 1978 Razorback Marching Band photographed in the outside theater of the Fine Arts Center on campus.

With a regular season record of 9-2, Holtz and the Hogs flew to Tempe, Arizona, to play in the Fiesta Bowl on December 25 against the UCLA Bruins. The Razorback Band did not attend, partly because it was played on Christmas Day and partly because of funding problems. The game ended in a 10–10 tie.

Though the right photo does not depict the Razorback Basketball Pep Band, this is a good place to mention that Jim Robken, a graduate student, undertook the responsibilities for the Pep Band as it grew in size. Eddie Sutton once again led the team to a tie for first place in the SWC, winning the SWC Tourney and making it to the third round of the NCAA Tournament in 1979.

The Flag Corps for 1979 was twenty-one members strong and choreographed by Jim Robken. For its single out-of-state football game that season the Razorback Band went to College Station for the 22–0 shutout that the Hogs handed to the Aggies. Bus trips to Little Rock or out-of-state games generally cost about twenty-seven thousand dollars per game at the time, and the travel was funded by the Athletic Department.

The 1979 majorette line was one of the largest group of twirlers the Razorback Band had fielded up until then. Kneeling in the front row center was Christy Grubb, the featured twirler who would retain that honor for the following two seasons. Drum majors for the year were Tony Logue and Alex Dunlap.

THE JANZEN YEARS, 1970–1985

The 250-plus-member 1979 Marching Razorback Band burst the seams of the existing Band Building built in 1964 for a maximum of 150 musicians. Janzen was quoted in the *Traveler* as saying, "It's like trying to fit them into a telephone booth." The band rehearsed its music in the outdoor Fine Arts Theater, weather permitting. Although Janzen submitted a statement of need to the administration for a new Band Building, he did not see it as being forthcoming in the next few years.

Although Arkansas defeated Texas in a close one played in War Memorial Stadium in 1979, Houston rained on the Hogs' parade the following weekend, knocking them out of the Cotton Bowl. With a 10-1 record, Arkansas played Alabama in the Sugar Bowl losing to the Crimson Tide 24–9. At the half (shown above) the Marching Razorbacks ended their presentation with a patriotic drill salute dedicated to the American hostages held in Iran with the fervent hope for their early release in the new year. Jimmy Carter had just lost his bid for re-election to Ronald Reagan, and the hostages were released three weeks after the Sugar Bowl game was played.

Back home in Fayetteville the basketball season was in full swing, and Robken's students vied to play in the Pep Band at the games (this was a far cry from earlier years when it was difficult to commit students to play). Sutton's roundballers finished the season with a 21-8 record, placing second in the SWC and again making it to the third round of the NCAA Tournament.

In addition to concerts played on campus by the Symphonic Band, the Concert Band, and the smaller ensembles during the school year, the Symphonic Band also played a special concert on April 13 in the Municipal Auditorium in Eureka Springs. That program included *Ballet Parisien Suite* by Offenbach and music from the film scores of *Fiddler on the Roof* and *Star Trek*.

Because ABC-TV and the NCAA rescheduled the 1980 Texas-Arkansas game to be played on Labor Day in order to get it on the television schedule, the contest turned out to be the earliest fall college game ever played to date. This also called for an early start of the Razorback Band's rehearsal plan on August 14 for a full band trip to Austin. Texas eventually won that contest 23–17, and the Hogs' second game of the season did not occur until three weeks later. Shown above (left to right) are Assistant Director Chalon Ragsdale, Special Assistant Jim Robken and Director of Bands Eldon Janzen. At left are drum majors Alex Dunlap (right) and Carl Mouton standing on either side of featured twirler Christy Grubb. On the following page is the group portrait of the entire Marching Razorback Band for 1980.

THE JANZEN YEARS, 1970–1985

These 1980 football-season photos above show the Marching Razorbacks backing up the cheerleaders at a pep rally in the Greek Theatre and performing during a halftime show.

The left photo captures a formation of the Marching Razorbacks that highlighted the halftime shows in 1980. Music played during the season included the theme from *Patton*, "Amazing Grace," "St. Louis Blues March," and "Alexander's Ragtime Band."

The Hogs finished the 1980 season 6-5 and accepted a bid to play in the Hall of Fame Bowl in Birmingham against Tulane on December 27. Rather than having the Razorback Band appear at the game, Eldon Janzen directed a local Birmingham high-school band playing Arkansas pep songs in the stands. Tulane won the game 34–15.

Once again in 1980–81 Eddie Sutton's basketball team finished first in the SWC and made it to the third round of the NCAA Big Dance. Jim Robken's basketball band, re-dubbed the Hogwild Band, picked up on Sutton's energy and claimed the *William Tell Overture* as the team's second fight song.

For 1981–82 Eldon Janzen served as the interim chair of the Music Department with Chal Ragsdale assuming the position of Director of Bands. Incorporated into the marching style that season were more angular and abstract formations than had been seen in the past. With the football schedule falling as it did, Ragsdale was able to design three completely new halftime shows without either show being performed before the same stadium audience twice. The photo above shows the Razorback Band marching to the "Semper Fidelis" portion of the standard pre-game show.

The left photo features the majorette line of the 250-member Razorback Band for 1981. Ragsdale's first halftime design centered on the march "Thunder and Blazes," Gene Krupa's version of "Sing, Sing, Sing," and the movie theme from *Superman.* The second show incorporated arrangements of music from *Star Wars, Raiders of the Lost Ark,* and *All That Jazz.* And the final set of shows showcased a medley of favorites including "Eternal Father," "This Is My Country," "My Country 'Tis of Thee," and "Battle Hymn of the Republic."

Announcements inviting former band members to return at Homecoming to perform in an alumni band had been modestly successful by 1981. One such individual to join in the fun in 1981 was Tom Tappan from Helena who had played saxophone in the band in 1927. Shown on this page are photos of Tappan from both years mentioned. (These photos previously appeared in Dr. Ethel Simpson's book *Image and Reflection.*)

With a 1981 regular season record of 8-3 (including an all-important win over Texas), the Hogs bagged an invitation to the Gator Bowl in Jacksonville against the North Carolina Tarheels. Because of a lack of funds, the Razorback Band did not attend the game (and no one substituted for them either). North Carolina won 31–27.

Robken's Hogwild Band shook the rafters of Barnhill during the 1981–82 season, cheering on the basketball team to the top of the SWC, to winning the SWC Tourney, and to playing in the first round of the NCAA Tournament. A popular tune for Arkansas fans arising that season was a variation of a Mac Davis hit that ended with, "Oh Lord, it's hard to be humble, when you're an Arkansas Razorback fan."

In early 1982 Dr. Arthur Tollefson from Northwestern University became the new chair of the U of A Music Department, thus allowing Eldon Janzen to resume his duties with the Razorback Band.

The 1982 football season began on a high note and continued on through the first seven games without a loss. Pep rallies were high-spirited with the Razorback Band joining in with its 220-member marching unit led by drum majors Steve Palen and Rusty Morris. With Eldon Janzen back in the director's chair, the band played at all the in-state games and took a road trip to Dallas for the SMU game.

Lou Holtz's coaching led the team to an 8-2-1 record for 1982 and earned the Hogs a berth in the final Bluebonnet Bowl in Houston on December 31. The coach is shown at right running with the team onto the field through the legs of the band's pre-game "A."

The U of A brass line right played at the 1982 Rice game encouraging the Hogs to "charge" the Owls. When the Razorback Band later appeared in Dallas to play SMU on November 20, the group stayed an extra day and marched at their first ever NFL football game when the Dallas Cowboys played Tampa Bay. Both games were played in Texas Stadium and featured the Marching Razorbacks at the half in drill maneuvers set to "Thunder and Blazes," "Tiger Rag," and "Georgia on My Mind."

The photo below is from a fall 1982 article in the *Houston Post* covering the bands of the SWC. Responding to the reporter's comments that the Arkansas Band tended to play "old hat tunes," Janzen responded, "You've got to realize that the folks who make the contributions to the Athletic Department and buy tickets are over 40 and they like more traditional music. As far as I'm concerned, that's what we'll play." But the writer also noted that "the Razorback Band is implementing innovative styles of marching into its program, like [drum-and-bugle] corp-style marching."

The Hogwild Band continued to incite the crowds and enthuse the basketball team through the successful 1982–83 season with the team amassing a 26-4 record and making it to the second round of the NCAA Tournament. Plastic hog hats mushroomed in appearance at the games.

Beginning in January of 1983, Eldon Janzen took a six-month leave of absence to write the book, *Band Director's Survival Guide* (published in 1985). Later, on May 1 at the annual band banquet, Preston and Kathryn Woodruff were honored for their thirty years as chaperones on Razorback Band football trips. The Woodruffs are shown right, first and third from the left, waiting to board for yet another Texas-Arkansas game with the band (note the "Austin" destination sign in the bus window).

The drummers at right get the students ready for the 1983 football season at the Tulsa pep rally. During the second weekend in October, which was an open date for the team, the Razorback Band marched in a parade in Bentonville that the town held in honor of its distinguished citizens, Sam and Helen Walton of Wal-Mart fame.

Though the football team had an up-and-down season in 1983, the Marching Razorbacks hung in there through the good and bad. An example of the bad was the SMU game in Little Rock that was played in a thundering downpour and tornado alert. Note band members in the ponchos above on the field during their halftime performance. A broader view of the band on the field at halftime shows the water standing on the Astroturf and the stands cleared of all but the most loyal band fans.

With the band's staff intact from previous years, Eldon Janzen welcomed back the 220-plus-member band for the 1983–84 season. New to the program was an acquisition that promised to make creating drill routines much easier and save a lot of time—a "marching" computer. With the new computer program Janzen stated, "that before, we would spend 90 percent of our time drawing the charts and 10 percent being creative. Now we spend 10 percent drawing and 90 percent being creative."

When the Hogs hosted the Houston Cougars during Legislative Weekend 1983, Leon McAuliffe played along with the Marching Razorbacks during the halftime show. He also played with the group during the previous week's Texas-Arkansas contest in Little Rock. Unfortunately the Hogs finished the season with a record of 6-5 and received no bowl offers. Coach Lou Holtz resigned shortly afterward. It is worthy to note that Holtz never had a losing season while at Arkansas.

In the photo at right the Dancing Razorback does his thing while the Hogwild Band takes to the floor playing "Hey, Look Me Over." Sutton's boys had another good year, finishing second in the SWC and going on to the NCAA Tournament (they lost in the first round). Their final record was 25-7.

Though the concert season for 1983–84 was excellent all year long, the final concert of the year was probably the most fun. On April 28 the Concert and Symphonic Bands combined forces into a 120-member unit for a concert on the Old Main lawn. Students and area citizens were invited to bring lawn chairs and blankets on which to sit, and picnics were encouraged. But the visual treat of the evening was James Saied (owner of Saied Music Company) conducting the band in a series of Sousa marches dressed like old John Philip himself.

The 1984 football season started out with a new head coach at the helm, Ken Hatfield, a former Razorback who came to Arkansas from the Air Force Academy. Nineteen eighty-four would also prove significant for the Razorback Band in that it was the last marching season that Eldon Janzen would serve as director of the marching unit. Janzen, however, remained on the staff as the Director of Bands for another decade. Janzen's drum majors for 1984 were Rusty Morris and Paul Simkins, and Patricia Van Ausdale performed as the featured twirler in front of the majorettes pictured left.

The students at near right are rehearsing for a 1984 halftime show, and the student at far right is displaying the results of those hours of practice during a halftime performance. In addition to the four Little Rock games and the three Fayetteville contests, the Razorback Band also performed at the Texas game played in Austin.

At the first two games of the 1984 season, three Marching Razorbacks, who had been chosen to march as part of the Olympic All-America Band at the XXIII Olympiad in Los Angeles the previous summer, were honored at the beginning of the Navy and Tulsa halftime shows. Those students were David Kirkley and John Ferguson on trumpet and Jeff Bright on tuba. The right photo was taken during the Tulsa show with the band marching a circle drill to Kenny Rogers's "She Believes in Me."

Rain was an uninvited guest at Homecoming 1984, but the Razorback Band donned ponchos and played through the precipitation. Note the raingear sported by audience members in the right photo. Halftime numbers to which the band marched that season included "Yakkety Percussion," "No Name Boogie," and "Big Noise from Winnetka." At the end of the season the football team (record 7-3-1) went to the Liberty Bowl in Memphis as did the Razorback Band. Auburn won the game 21–15.

Photos on this page document the members of Lambda Chapter of Kappa Kappa Psi (above) and Psi Chapter of Tau Beta Sigma for 1984–85.

Razorback basketball was as hot on campus in 1984–85 as it had been in previous years, though the team lost more games than in any previous year under Eddie Sutton's leadership (22-13 overall). But a real shocker came at the end of the season when Sutton announced his leaving to become the head coach of the University of Kentucky.

After having served as the interim director of the Marching Razorback Band during the year that Janzen became the interim chair of the Music Department, Chalon Ragsdale accepted the full directorship of the group in 1985 when Janzen relinquished that position. Ragsdale had been hired as percussion instructor and assistant director of the Razorback Band in 1975 and has been most recognized over his years spent at the University of Arkansas for his skill in arranging performance numbers to which the band has marched at halftime shows. A graduate of Auburn and East Carolina Universities, Ragsdale was most meticulous in his planning of band performances, and his expectations were as high as his arrangements were dynamic. Though he only held the director's position of the Marching Razorbacks for two years, he conducted the Concert Band, the Symphonic Band, and the Wind Ensemble for a number of seasons. But his real home has always been with the percussion section and mentoring those students to perform at their highest levels.

After ceding the Marching Razorbacks' director's position, Ragsdale returned to his previous duties of percussion instructor and arranger and eventually served as the chair of the Music Department from 1990 to 1998. As of this printing, his current titles include Professor of Percussion and Director of the Percussion Ensemble.

Taking over the reins of the Marching Razorbacks from Ragsdale in 1987 was Jim Robken, who first joined the University of Arkansas band program in the late 1970s as a graduate student. Soon he was responsible for directing the basketball Pep Band at home games in Barnhill Field House and choreographing the flag line for the Marching Razorbacks. When the opportunity arose to add the Marching Razorbacks to his list of responsibilities, he grabbed it and ran. In fact running became almost a trademark movement for Robken during his stay in the athletic bands' director's chair. Within a few seasons of directing the basketball Pep Band he renamed the group the "Hogwild Band" and became a legend stirring up the fans in the Field House to the strains of *The William Tell Overture* and galloping around the building wearing a Lone Ranger Mask. And during the football season he carried many of the antics that had worked successfully around the basketball court to the sidelines of the football field.

During the four years that Robken directed the Marching Razorbacks, the Hogwild Band, and Concert Band, he was always

CHAPTER 10

The Ragsdale-Robken Years

1985–1991

looking for a new hook with which to grab the fans, be it a new way to enter the field or the rewriting the lyrics to a popular tune to fit Hog fans' needs. ("Oh Lord, it's hard to be humble, when you're an Arkansas Razorback fan.")

Though a number of reasons have been postulated as to why Robken left his job after the spring of 1991, he stated to the press that "you get to a point in life where you want to do other things." Soon afterward, he accepted the position as Director of Bands at his undergraduate alma mater, Louisiana Tech, and was off to Ruston.

Chalon Ragsdale and Jim Robken brought very different approaches to their direction of the Razorback Bands during their times. And the very best parts of each richly added to the legacy passed on to their successors.

Chalon Ragsdale took over as director of the Marching Razorbacks for the fall of 1985 with Jim Robken as his assistant and Robert Bright continuing as the Voice of the Razorback Band. Paul Simkins and Sandy Stephenson served as drum majors and Leah Jo Brogden and Marvin Rackleff enjoyed the limelight as the band's new featured twirlers. The two photos on this page reflect the two styles of uniforms that the band wore at games depending upon the weather.

The photos on this page illustrate the complex drills and formations that the Marching Razorbacks executed during the 1985 season. For the band's foray into Texas that season, the group went to Fort Worth for the TCU game.

With a 9-2 record in 1985 (the losses were to Texas and Texas A & M) the Hogs were invited to play Arizona State in the Holiday Bowl in San Diego on December 20. The band flew to the game from Tulsa and performed a patriotic show at the half dedicated to the American Armed Forces serving throughout the world. Arkansas won the nail-biter 18–17.

Nolan Richardson was named the new Razorback basketball coach for 1985–86, and his team finished the year with a slump-ending 12-16 record. Robken and the Hogwild Band worked hard all season at keeping everyone's spirits up.

During the 1985–86 concert season, three members of the Razorback Band were chosen to serve in the Liberty Band the following summer in New York—Kevin Miller, Cathy Matson, and Stan Barnhill. They were part of the five-hundred-member Liberty Band celebrating the unveiling of the newly renovated Statue of Liberty in special parades and concerts on Liberty Island.

In his second year as director of the Marching Razorbacks, Chal Ragsdale welcomed back Leah Jo Brogden as the band's featured twirler (shown above center) and signed up Tom Nelson and Mike Ferguson as his new drum majors. For the third time in as many years, the 1986 season began with the band traveling to Fort Smith to march in the city's Great Raft Race Parade in support of the local United Way.

For 1986 the football season was played without a single open date and with the first five games played in the state. Also the Razorback Band traveled to Austin for the sixth game played against Texas. That accounted for six consecutive weeks of halftime shows requiring enough variation in drills to prevent a lot of duplication of performances.

Marching drills for 1986 included patterns performed to the tunes "Puttin' on the Ritz," "Who's Johnny?" and the march "Thunder and Blazes" as shown in these two photos. The Tulsa show (top photo) ended in the formation at bottom with a salute to Arkansas's Sesquicentennial Celebration (150th birthday) to the music of "Arkansas, You Run Deep in Me." With a record of 9-2 for the regular season, the football team was invited to the Orange Bowl in Miami, but the Sooners were prepared for the Hogs on that New Year's Day in 1987 and beat the Hogs 42–8. The band rode to and from Miami in a five-bus caravan and performed their polished "Superman," "Elk's Parade," and "Who's Johnny?" drills during the halftime extravaganza.

In Nolan Richardson's second season, the basketball team improved over the previous year (19-14 overall) and made it to the second round of the National Invitational Tournament. Through it all the Hogwild Band poured on the excitement, and Robken, wearing a Long Ranger mask, continued to incite the crowd, running around Barnhill Arena and waving his arms while the band played *The William Tell Overture.*

The concert season at the University of Arkansas had over the years evolved from being a spring semester series of events to a school-year-long calendar of events. For 1986–87 various public performances took place on campus from November through May. For example, a November concert included presentations by the Concert Wind Ensemble, the Trumpet Ensemble, the Flute Ensemble, the Percussion Ensemble, the Double Reed Ensemble, the Clarinet Choir, and the Tuba and Trombone Ensembles. And at the April 16 concert Janzen and Ragsdale conducted the Symphonic and Concert Bands respectively in a program presented in the Arkansas Union Ballroom.

In the fall of 1987 Jim Robken was the new director of the Razorback Marching Band as well as the leader of the Hogwild Band. Chal Ragsdale opted to return to his previous duties as percussion instructor and music arranger for the band. Robken's student leaders included drum majors Mike Ferguson and Kevin Miller, who fronted the band with eleven majorettes and two featured twirlers.

Halftime shows for 1987 included a salute to the two-hundredth anniversary of the U. S. Constitution and a Homecoming celebration which also was Band Day (with nineteen area high-school bands in attendance at the game) and Parent's Day on campus. The photo at right shows the banner that preceded the Razorback Band in the Homecoming Parade that year.

The Texas-Arkansas game in 1987 was played in Little Rock and broadcast over ESPN. The photos right taken of the Razorback Band's halftime show at that game illustrate the interesting shape of the drill formations during the season. Music featured during the shows included "Amazing Grace," "America the Beautiful," and music from the movie *E.T.*

For the full band's annual trip to Texas in 1987, the group marched at the Texas A & M game in College Station. The Pep Band also made it to other out-of-state-games, save for the University of Hawaii game played in Honolulu.

The Razorback Band could be counted on to support the team from the stands during the games as well as march during pre-game ceremonies and at halftime. The photo at left shows band members up in arms at a 1987 game. With an 8-4 record the Hogs went to the Liberty Bowl in post-season play, where the Marching Razorbacks performed on what drum major Mike Ferguson said was "the coldest night I ever marched in all my high school and college band days."

The highlight of the 1988 concert season was the selection of the Symphonic Band to portray the role of the famous Sousa Concert Band for benefit appearances sponsored by the Rotary Clubs in Oklahoma City and Tulsa. The occasions were the celebration of Congress's declaration of "Stars and Stripes Forever" being named the U. S. National March. The music was prepared by Director Janzen and conducted by James G. Saied, well-known Sousa impersonator in traditional "Sousa-style" concerts. The announcer-narrator was none other than John Philip Sousa III, grandson of the world-famous bandleader. The university bandsmen were appropriately dressed in vintage Sousa band uniforms and played to packed houses, featuring traditional marches and concert selections from the original Sousa band repertoire.

In 1988 the Marching Razorbacks received their first uniform makeover since 1975 with a red bolero jacket worn over a black cummerbund and white trousers topped off with a West Point–styled hat and white feathery plume.

Leading the Razorback Band on the field for 1988–89 were drum majors Kevin Miller and Marsha Wilson. With appearances at six of the in-state games and at the Texas game in Austin, the band witnessed much Hog success on the gridiron that year. By the time of the kick-off of the final regular season game against the University of Miami, the Razorbacks had racked up a 10-0 record. And although the Hogs lost that last game to the defending national champions 18–16, they retained their number eight national ranking and still went to the Cotton Bowl.

*Mobil Cotton Bowl
Dallas 1989*

The 1989 Cotton Bowl pitted the Razorbacks against the UCLA Bruins, and both schools brought their bands to the game. At the half the Marching Razorbacks marched their polished "Sounds of the Southwest" show from earlier in the season, featuring drills set to the soundtrack music of *The Magnificent Seven* and *Silverado*. The Bruins won the game 17–3.

Razorback basketball kept improving in 1988–89 as the team captured the top spot in the SWC and finally won the SWC Tournament before making it to the third round of the NCAA Tournament. And the Hogwild Band was there through it all.

A bright spot in the 1988–89 concert season was the Arkansas Low Brass Symposium held on campus, coordinated by Gerald Sloan and Paul Johnston. Great drawing cards were guest appearances by former U of A bandsman and graduate Dr. Jerry Young, tuba virtuoso from the faculty of the University of Wisconsin at Eau Claire, and Dr. Vern Kagarice, trombone virtuoso from the University of North Texas.

For 1989–90 the 220-member Razorback Band was fronted by drum majors Caryn Hobson and Shane Jones and featured twirlers Andrea Whitaker and Renessa Dunlap. Again the band was so large that music rehearsals for the entire group had to be held outside, as pictured at right, in the Fine Arts outdoor theater, weather permitting.

Adding a whimsical touch to its 1989 halftime repertoire, the Razorback Band marched a show featuring music from Saturday morning television cartoons and Walt Disney animated feature films. Such tunes included the *Flintstones* theme and the songs, "It's a Small, Small World," and "When You Wish upon a Star."

Also in 1989 there was an increased use of kaleidoscopic type drills by the Razorback Band (as shown in the photos on this page) emulating the very popular drum-and-bugle-corps style sweeping the country.

The Marching Razorbacks also had the opportunity to march at their second NFL game when they were invited in 1989 to appear at a Dallas Cowboy game the day after the band performed at the Texas A & M game in College Station. During regular season play, the Hogs won all their games save for the Texas contest, at which band members Buddy Johnson, Monte Womble, and Kevin Hunter above express their dissatisfaction.

With their 10-1 record, the Hogs once again returned to the Cotton Bowl in 1990 for their second back-to-back appearance there in the team's history (the previous times were the Cotton Bowl games of 1965 and 1966). After the Razorback Band marched in the Cotton Bowl Parade (shown above), the group reprised their well-received drills from earlier shows (to Stravinski's "Firebird" and Kabelevsky's "Comedians Gallop") during halftime. A short time after Tennessee defeated the Hogs, Ken Hatfield signed a contract becoming the new head coach at Clemson. Assistant Jack Crowe ascended to the head coaching position at Arkansas a few days later.

Among other concert season presentations in 1989–90, the U of A Symphonic Band and the University of Central Arkansas Symphonic Band performed a joint program on February 22 in the Arkansas Union Ballroom and later repeated the concert on the Conway campus in Waldran Auditorium on March 8.

Important for the athletic teams and affecting the Razorback Band program as a byproduct was the Southeastern Conference's vote in May 1990 to expand its membership from ten to twelve schools. Soon the U of A was invited to join the fold. The result was that Arkansas would continue playing the 1990 and 1991 football seasons as part of the SWC and begin playing as part of the SEC in the fall of 1992. The remaining sports teams, including basketball, would start competing as conference members against SEC teams beginning in the fall of 1991.

With the U of A moving to the SEC in 1992, director of the Marching Razorbacks Jim Robken declared the 1990 and 1991 football seasons as being Arkansas's farewell tour from the SWC. Bandsman Stewart Bryan (below) and the other 220 members of the Razorback Band marched at all five of the first games played in-state, at the Texas game in Austin, and at two of the last five games that were played within Arkansas's borders. Sadly, the Hogs lost seven games in a row that season leading to a 1990 record of 3-8.

Drum majors Shane Jones and Scott Howard are shown leading the band into Razorback Stadium for the 1990 contest with the Golden Hurricane of Tulsa. Notice the newly completed Broyles Complex in the north end zone of Razorback Stadium in the lower photo.

The left photo from the fall of 1990 was taken of the Marching Razorbacks performing the "G-O H-O-G-S" formation in War Memorial Stadium. Halftime shows featured such music as Chuck Mangione's "Days of Harvest" and "La Virta de la Canta" and the classics "Ride of the Valkeries" by Wagner, "Dance in Time" by Korsakov, and The 1812 Overture by Tchaikovsky. One show also had a patriotic theme dedicated to the soldiers serving at the time in Operation Desert Shield in the Middle East.

The 1990 Razorback percussion section marches to the strains of "Batman" during one of their "Action Super-Heros" halftime shows. Another drill in the show gave equal time to "Superman."

A view from the press box follows up the previous photo regarding the "Action Super-Heros" show. Note the outline of the trademarked bat on the field. Robken also reminded the crowd of the U of A's impending switch from the SWC to the SEC by having the band play "Lord, It's Hard to be Humble" and "All My Ex's Live in Texas" even at the close of a 3-8 season coached by Jack Crowe.

A short while after the basketball team finished its incredible 1990–91 season (ending first in the SWC, winning the SWC tourney, and ascending to the Elite Eight at the NCAA Tournament), Hogwild Band and Marching Razorback director Jim Robken resigned his positions at the University of Arkansas. He subsequently took a job as Director of Bands at his undergraduate alma mater, Louisiana Tech.

In the wake of Jim Robken's leaving in 1991, the Music Department at the University of Arkansas set out to find the right person to helm the Marching Razorback Band and found him in W. Dale Warren. Warren came to Arkansas from the University of Kentucky where he had served five years as associate director of bands after having conducted championship marching and symphonic bands on the Kentucky secondary-school level. With a master's in music education from the University of Kentucky, Warren was also an accomplished computer drill-design clinician.

In his nine years directing the Marching Razorbacks and four seasons leading the Hogwild Band, a number of unprecedented events occurred that once again thrust the bands into the national limelight and even involved some international travel. The election of Arkansas's Bill Clinton to the presidency sent the Marching Razorbacks to Washington, D.C., to march in the 1993 inaugural parade. When the Razorback basketball team made it to the NCAA Final Four in back-to-back appearances in 1994 and 1995, the Hogwild Band was there for most of the rides (especially in 1994 when the team won the national championship). Then there was the invitation for the Razorback Band to march in the 1997 Saint Patrick's Day parade in Dublin, Ireland, and to appear as a special guest band at the Limerick International Marching Band Competition (about half the band was fortunate enough to go on that trip). And the real icing on the cake was when the Wind Symphony was granted the opportunity to play in Carnegie Hall in April of 2000 as part of the Distinguished Ensemble Debut Series.

Although the football team had its ups and downs in the 1990s as the new kids on the Southeastern Conference block, the band was able to accompany the team on four memorable trips during that time: the 1995 SEC Championship Game played in Atlanta, the 1995 CarQuest Bowl held in Miami, the 1999 Citrus Bowl in Orlando, and the 2000 Cotton Bowl that rematched Texas and Arkansas (the Hogs won 27–6).

A building boom exploded on the U of A campus and in Fayetteville during the 1990s from which the Razorback Bands were able to benefit. The new Walton Arts Center opened on Dickson Street in 1992 where the band began to perform its concerts in the Baum Walker Hall. A new basketball complex, Bud Walton Arena, had its grand opening in 1993, which had brought about a "Good Bye

CHAPTER 11

The Warren-Gunter Years

1991–2004

Tour" to Barnhill Arena the previous season. The band also played for the reopening ceremonies of Old Main in 1991 after a multi-year refurbishing that tallied in the millions of dollars. But the building that most directly caused smiles to break out on band members' faces was the new Lewis E. Epley Jr. Hall, the new band building (1997) named after the chair of the University of Arkansas Trustees and former Voice of the Razorback Band.

A number of significant milestones for the university and for the band in particular occurred during W. Dale Warren's tenure. The university celebrated one hundred years of football on its campus, the U of A itself passed its 125th anniversary of existence as did the Razorback Band, and the Lambda Chapter of Kappa Kappa Psi held a special banquet in honor of its seventy-fifth anniversary of service to the band. And two long-time Music Department faculty members with a rich history of connections to the band retired, Eldon Janzen in 1995 and Robert Bright in 1998.

Among the many significant contributions that Warren made to the Razorback Band program included the introduction of a new tradition to the band calendar with the Band Spectacular concerts signaling an end to the marching season with a presentation of all the halftime-show and spirit-song musical arrangements performed during the fall. And to make sure that everyone had an opportunity to recapture those sounds for posterity, at least two compact disc releases were made available during his tenure at the helm.

When Warren handed off the baton of the Marching Razorbacks in 2000, Timothy Gunter took it, fulfilling a dream he had had since he was a child. As Gunter told the press at the time of his being named the group's new director, "as an eighth grader, I remember telling both my band teacher and my mother I was one day going to be the director of the Razorback Marching Band. Here I am." And indeed he was, and in his inaugural season, the organization passed the 300-member mark for the first time in the school's history with 318 band students marching in the fall of 2000. A graduate of the University of Arkansas with both his bachelor's and master's degrees, Gunter preceded his faculty position at Arkansas as the Associate Director of Bands and Director of Athletic Bands at Rutgers University. By the time he assumed the director's job of the Marching Razorbacks in 2000, he had already been assistant director for the group and director of the Hogwild and

Symphonic Bands for five years. From the fall of 2000 he has been the Director of Athletic Bands, and W. Dale Warren has been the Director of Concert Bands. Martin Reynolds served as Gunter's assistant director for the 2000–2001 school year, and Jeremy Pratchard has filled that position up to the time of this printing.

As this publication goes to press and another school year begins, there is no doubt that both Warren and Gunter will continue to impress upon their band students the importance, responsibility and pride that being a part of the University of Arkansas brings with it.

To open the 1991 football and marching season the new Razorback Band director, W. Dale Warren, retained the traditional pre-game flavor, music, and style from previous years that fans had long enjoyed and expected. The "Arkansas Fight Song," the Hog calls, "Semper Fidelis," the national anthem, the Arkansas alma mater, and the "Big A" sequence were all there.

The majorettes above were joined in front of the 240-member band in 1991 by drum majors Scott Howard and Matthew Pratt, along with featured twirler Renessa Dunlap. The new director, W. Dale Warren, came to Arkansas from the University of Kentucky where he had served as associate director for five years and completed his master's degree in music education.

As a proponent of contemporary marching with abstract curves, lines, and circles encompassing the field, Warren designed the 1991 half-time shows with those in mind. Music used during the season included a patriotic salute to soldiers recently returned from Operation Desert Storm and a medley of tunes honoring George Gershwin. The left photo was taken of the Arkansas Band at the Houston game played in Fayetteville during Homecoming.

On October 19, 1991, in Little Rock at the final Texas-Arkansas game played between those two rivals as members of the SWC, both teams' bands were in attendance and pulled out all the stops with their performances. And the Hogs put an exclamation point on the nationally televised game by winning 14–13.

Toward the end of the 1991 season the Razorback Pep Band accompanied the team to Lubbock and witnessed the Hogs' defeat by the Red Raiders 38–21. To add insult to injury, the University of Arkansas administration stated that because of insurance reasons or some such story that Pep Band members could go to the game, but that they could not take their instruments or represent the university. Reports indicated that fifty band members sat together at the game dressed in specially made T-shirts and played the "Arkansas Fight Song" on kazoos throughout the game.

Despite having a 6-5 record under Coach Jack Crowe, Arkansas received a bid to play Georgia in the 1991 Independence Bowl in Shreveport on December 29. Shown at right is the Arkansas Band at the half performing their "Spanish Spectacular" show featuring the music of "Malaga," "Malaguena," and "Children of Sanchez." The Bulldogs won the game 24–15.

In their first season in the SEC, the Runnin' Razorbacks under Nolan Richardson took first place in the regular season race and made it to the second round of the NCAA Big Dance.

Perhaps the brightest night of the 1992 spring concert season was on April 28 when the Symphonic and Concert Bands presented their inaugural concert in the new Walton Arts Center on Dickson Street.

By any standard, the 1992–93 U of A school year was a frenetic one for the Razorback Band. Coach Crowe was in for one game and then out after the loss to AA Citadel. Then Joe Kines took over until Danny Ford signed on officially at the end of the football season. Arkansas governor Bill Clinton was elected president of the United States, and the band marched in his inaugural parade. Warren and the Marching Razorbacks began a new tradition by performing a season-ending concert called the annual Band Spectacular in the Walton Arts Center. And on top of that the basketball team had a great winning season making it to the third round of the NCAA Tournament, while at the same time playing a good-bye tour to Barnhill Arena with the new Bud Walton Arena slated to open the next season. And of course, the concert season overlapped both semesters.

The Razorback Band for 1992–93 was 223-members strong and marched halftime shows that season to themes spotlighting songs celebrating New York City, *The Wizard of Oz*, and *The Wiz*, and tunes saluting "American Patriotism."

Sean Campbell (left) plays to the upper tiers and Katherine Seamon and Kim Shepherd (below right) enthuse those more on eye level during a Razorback football game. New to the band staff in 1992 was the addition of Connie Vick as the indispensable band secretary and "Band Mom."

With Arkansas governor Bill Clinton running for president in 1992, the Razorback Band joined him at a political rally on campus in the fall, and the candidate played along on tenor sax when the band struck up the "Arkansas Fight Song." (Bill Clinton attended band camp at the U of A in the early 1960s.)

Baum Walker Hall in the Walton Arts Center was the site of the first annual Band Spectacular that the Razorback Band held on November 17, 1992. The concert featured Razorback spirit songs and cadences plus music played during the season's halftime shows.

At the inauguration of President Bill Clinton the Razorback Band proudly marched down Pennsylvania Avenue past the reviewing stand in front of the White House on January 20, 1993, enduring very cold temperatures.

While in Washington, D.C., for the inaugural ceremonies, the Razorback Band also took time to pose on the steps of the U.S. Capitol. On the front row are featured twirlers Renessa Dunlap and Ginger Glover and drum majors Matthew Pratt and Scott Howard. Director of Bands Eldon Janzen is at the lower left of the picture.

The 1992–93 Razorback basketball team ended their winning season by making it to the third round of the NCAA Tournament. Shown at left is the Hogwild Band at the NCAA East Regional in Winston-Salem, North Carolina.

The final game played in Barnhill Arena by the men's Razorback basketball team was held on March 3, 1993, with the Hogs defeating LSU for the SEC Western Conference Championship. After the game, many dignitaries associated with the team over the years including former Hogwild Band director Jim Robken (in the Panama hat in the above photo) gave speeches and recalled special memories regarding the building. Afterwards the evening would be designated as "The Night the Lights Went Out in Barnhill."

At the first pep rally for the 1993 Razorback football team, new head coach Danny Ford introduced his squad of players who went on and amassed a 6-4-1 season record. Later in the year it was discovered that Alabama had fielded an ineligible player, resulting in a victory being given to the Hogs.

During one of the trips to play a game in Little Rock in the fall of 1993 the 220-member Razorback Band took some time to pose for the above photo on the steps of the State Capitol. Shown in the front row are drum majors Matthew Pratt and Chris Cansler and featured twirlers Ginger Glover and Alia Harris. New on the band staff that year was assistant director Anthony Falcone.

The 1993 tuba section of the Marching Razorbacks is shown at left rehearsing their parts for a halftime show in Razorback Stadium. The shows that season featured the Oscar-winning soundtrack music of John Williams, selections from the musical *West Side Story*, and a tribute to master blues bands. The band's out-of-state trip that year took them to Jackson, Mississippi, for the Ole Miss game.

The Razorback Band hosted two large Band Days in 1993 with the first involving twenty-seven central Arkansas secondary-school bands at the Mississippi State game in Little Rock and the second (shown left) showcasing thirty Ozark Mountain–area bands during the Tulsa game in Fayetteville.

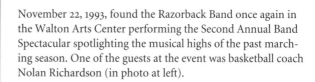

November 22, 1993, found the Razorback Band once again in the Walton Arts Center performing the Second Annual Band Spectacular spotlighting the musical highs of the past marching season. One of the guests at the event was basketball coach Nolan Richardson (in photo at left).

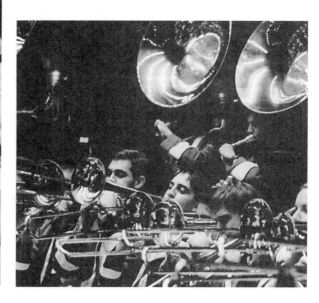

The 1993–94 Razorback basketball season was the one that fans of the Hogs remember with a smile. Bud Walton Arena held its grand opening, and President and Mrs. Clinton showed up the night Arkansas blew away Texas Southern 129–63. But more notably the team went all the way to win the national championship at the NCAA Tournament in Charlotte, North Carolina, defeating Duke in the title game, 76–72. The Hogwild Band was along for that fateful ride with W. Dale Warren directing the group (shown left at the 1994 SEC Tournament).

By the spring semester of 1994 the University of Arkansas band program boasted a record number of students interested in quality music. As a result three bands rehearsed for non-athletic performances—the Symphonic Band, the Concert Band, and the Campus Band. In February the Symphonic Band took to the road playing special concerts at Richardson (Texas) High School and at the Southwest Divisional Conference of Band Directors National Association on the Baylor campus.

In order to perform the quality of music expected for the halftime shows in 1994, members of the Razorback Band had to endure practicing their shows on the parking lot of Baldwin Music Company miles away from the U of A campus (see photo at left). Apparently Coach Danny Ford found the band's music distracting to his football players who practiced on nearby fields, so the band moved. And the band played on, as shown in the bottom photo focusing on Sean Campbell and his fellow trumpeters.

The 1994 Razorback Band took to the field 281 members strong that season with one featured twirler, Ginger Glover, and three drum majors, Matthew Pratt, Chris Cansler, and Doug Blevins. Also on board was a new Voice of the Marching Razorbacks— Mike Nail. That fall the band marched a record 111 music majors in the organization.

The 1994 Arkansas football season marked the one hundredth anniversary of Razorback football, and a logo recognizing the occasion was prominently painted in the center of the fields of both Razorback Stadium and War Memorial Stadium. Also note in the photo at right that the "Big A" formation for the pregame introduction of the football team stretched seventy yards from the far end-zone to the opposite forty-yard line.

Music featured during the Marching Razorbacks' 1994 halftime shows centered around a "Tribute to the Music of Stan Kenton" and the soundtrack music of the highly successful James Bond movies. The out-of-state game to which the band traveled that year was the Memphis State game played in Memphis.

One halftime show marched in 1994 celebrated the "100 Years of Razorback Football" with "A-R-K-A-N-S-A-S" spelled out and the unfurling of a large American flag. Ford's team finished the year 4-7. The basketball team did much better making it once again to the NCAA finals, but UCLA took home the crown, downing the Hogs 89–78 in Seattle.

Nineteen ninety-five marked a milestone for the Razorback Band with the retirement of Eldon Janzen as Director of Bands. A celebration of his twenty-five years in that position was held at the Fayetteville Hilton on July 13 at a gala attended by a crowd of well-wishers that included his peers and many current and former band members. At the first Fayetteville game of the 1995 season against South Carolina, the marching Razorbacks spelled out "J-A-N-Z-E-N" in tribute to him. As of this writing, he holds the title of Director of Bands Emeritus.

The right photo shows the Razorback Band's percussion section at a 1995 pep rally in the Greek Theatre on the Fayetteville campus. That season the band was composed of 286 members under the field direction of a record four drum majors—Chris Cansler, Shane Jennings, Tonya Blevins, and Landon Shockey. And the new Voice of the Marching Razorback Band was Larry Shank.

The photo at left shows members of the Marching Razorbacks waiting to go on at halftime during Homecoming 1995. After the game the band's equipment truck rolled backward down a hill beside the stadium and crashed into several other vehicles. Fortunately the human injuries were not serious, though a bit of band equipment was damaged.

The Razorback Band's half-time shows for 1995 were built around the music of a number of Walt Disney animated films *(Beauty and the Beast, Aladdin),* the sounds of "Great Horn Bands of the 1970s" (Earth Wind and Fire; Blood, Sweat and Tears; and Tower of Power), and favorite tunes of the 1960s ("Classical Gas," "Eleanor Rigby," and "Aquarius").

The 1995 Razorback football team won the SEC West Division and played Florida in Atlanta on December 2 for the SEC Championship. For their out-of-state game that year, the band bused it to the championship game and performed their "Great Horn Bands of the 1970s" show. Florida won the game 34–3.

Having gone 8-4 on the year, the Razorbacks received an invitation to play in the CarQuest Bowl against North Carolina in Miami on December 30. The band flew to that game where once again they performed their "Great Horn Bands of the 1970s" show and watched the Tarheels win out over the Hogs 20–10.

On February 28 the Wind Symphony had the unique opportunity in playing for the first day of issue of a new postage stamp commemorating the fiftieth anniversary of the establishment of the Fulbright Scholarships, created by former University of Arkansas president and U. S. senator J. William Fulbright.

As for the 1995–96 Razorback basketball team, they finished 20-13 on the year and made it to the third round of the Big Dance in what many called "one heck of a rebuilding year." The Hogwild Band was under the direction of a new director in Tim Gunter, himself a former Razorback bandsman and graduate assistant who was also on board as the Marching Razorbacks' associate director.

In 1996 the Razorback football team went 4-7 for the year under Coach Danny Ford presenting quite a challenge for W. Dale Warren and the band in keeping the fans' spirits up. Led by drum majors Chris Cansler, Shane Jennings, and Rocky Long, the 269-member Marching Razorback Band performed at all seven of the in-state games that year without being able to travel to any away games. Halftime shows centered around "Music For All America" highlighting great moments in American history, and also a "Spanish Spectacular" featuring "Pictures of Spain," "One More Time Chuck Corea" and "Children of Sanchez." (Jim Robken [former director of the Razorback Band] directed his Louisiana Tech band that marched and played at the Louisiana Tech–Arkansas game in Little Rock on October 12.)

Although the Arkansas basketball team had its worst season since 1985 in 1996–97 (18-18), Nolan Richardson led the guys to the semifinals of the NIT in the spring. Shown right is Tim Gunter leading the Hogwild Band at a game in Bud Walton Arena.

The concert season at the University of Arkansas found the majority of its programs performed in Baum Walker Hall of the Walton Arts Center in 1996–97. In the right photo W. Dale Warren conducts the Wind Symphony during the All-Bands Concert presented on February 24.

After an ambitious "Dollars for Dublin" fundraising campaign had been successfully completed, about half of the Marching Razorback Band was able to honor an invitation that had been extended to the group to march in the Saint Patrick's Day Parade in Dublin, Ireland, during March of 1997. Besides participating in the parade (shown below) the band also marched as a guest in the Limerick International Marching Band Competition.

After many years of suffering through inadequate space and other discomforts, the Razorback Band finally was able to utilize and dedicate a new band facility on the U of A campus on May 4, 1997. By remodeling the older building and expanding its size more than threefold, the structure was able to accommodate the full three-hundred-member band under its roof. At the dedication ceremony, the building was named after the then chair of the board of trustees and former Voice of the Razorback Band—Lewis E. Epley Jr. Also the main rehearsal hall was named for Eldon Janzen, Director of Bands Emeritus. Those two gentlemen are shown below cutting the ribbon.

Mirroring the 4-7 record of the previous year, the 1997 Razorback football team scored one hundred fewer points than its opponents in Danny Ford's last year as head coach. But the Razorback Band tried to remain focused on supporting the team with strong musical presentations during the fall. Marching again only at home games in Little Rock and Fayetteville, the band presented halftime shows featuring John Williams's *Star Wars* movie themes, a tribute to the thirtieth anniversary of the Blood Sweat and Tears rock group, and a visit back to the Disco Music of the 1970s ("The Hustle," "Saturday Night Fever," and a Village People medley). The above photo was taken at Homecoming during halftime.

Also at Homecoming '97, alumni members of past Razorback Bands returned to participate during the pre-game show and play with the Marching Razorbacks in the stands during the game.

The left photo taken from the press box in Razorback Stadium records a formation created by the Marching Razorbacks at the Mississippi State game (which Arkansas won 17–7). Leading the 273-member band on the field for 1997 were drum majors Shane Jennings, Rocky Long, and Shawn O'Kelley. Kendra Wilson was the featured twirler that season.

Basketball rebounded at the U of A in 1997–98 with the team going 24-9 on the season and once more receiving a bid to the NCAA Tournament (the guys made it to the second round). Hogwild Band director Tim Gunter (shown with band members at right) really put the group through its paces that season because (as he was quoted in the *Morning News*), "We get the best seats in the house. We need to earn them." With 135 students on the Pep Band's roster, anywhere from 40 to 70 members played at the men's basketball games and the women's basketball and volleyball games.

Concert season for 1997–98 as usual covered the entire school year with the Wind Symphony dominating the fall semester and the Symphonic and Concert Bands performing during the spring semester. Also in March, Anthony Falcone presented the Percussion Ensemble in its March Mallet Madness concert, featuring vibraphone recording artist, Jon Metzger.

On April 15, 1998, Robert Bright was honored at a concert in the Walton Arts Center for his twenty-nine years of teaching brass instruments at the University of Arkansas. His tenure also included a quarter century of serving as the Voice of the Razorback Band. At the concert sixty trumpet and twelve French horn players returned to perform for him one more time prior to his official retirement. As of this writing, he continues to teach private lessons.

For 1998–99 the Razorback Band received new uniforms shown at right which Warren described as "nothing short of dazzling." It was their first new look in ten years. Also new that season was the addition of another featured twirler with Jennifer Gosnell joining Kendra Wilson on the field.

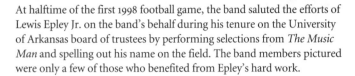

At halftime of the first 1998 football game, the band saluted the efforts of Lewis Epley Jr. on the band's behalf during his tenure on the University of Arkansas board of trustees by performing selections from *The Music Man* and spelling out his name on the field. The band members pictured were only a few of those who benefited from Epley's hard work.

Though Director W. Dale Warren and Assistant Director Tim Gunter are expressing mirth (above) because of a particularly successful concert presentation that year, they were equally pleased when Houston Nutt was named as the new head football coach in 1998. It would turn out to be a most successful season for both the team and the Marching Razorbacks.

The fall of 1998 was also the fiftieth anniversary of the completion of War Memorial Stadium in Little Rock. Besides marching a patriotic show accompanied by a fly-over of vintage and state-of-the-art aircraft to commemorate the event, the Razorback Band also presented shows that season in Little Rock and Fayetteville built around classic rock featuring guest soloist David Ragsdale of the group Kansas, and a "Sinatra Salute" showcasing the hits "My Way," "New York, New York," and "Luck Be a Lady."

Ending the regular season with the best record that an Arkansas team had posted in the 1990s (9-2), the Hogs accepted a bid to play Michigan in the Citrus Bowl in Orlando on January 1, 1999. The Razorback Band is seen at left marching their "Sinatra Salute" halftime show at the game. The Wolverines won the game with a final score of 45–31.

While at the 1999 Citrus Bowl, the Marching Razorbacks also had the opportunity to perform at Disney World in the Main Street Parade on national television.

One of the many concerts played during both semesters at the U of A in 1998–99 was the All-Bands Concert played in Baum Walker Hall on February 23 featuring the Symphonic Band, the Concert Band, and the Wind Symphony.

Of special note, the Lambda Chapter of Kappa Kappa Psi celebrated its seventy-fifth anniversary of service to the Razorback Band on June 5, 1999, at a special banquet at the Fayetteville Hilton. Dr. Richard Worthington returned as a special guest for the event, and Bill Woolly, David Woolly, Don King, and Sanford Tollette received special alumni awards for their past service to the band. The occasion also marked the 125th anniversary of the University of Arkansas Razorback Band.

In addition to raising the rafters of Bud Walton Arena from their special platform in the stands, the Hogwild Band took to the court on occasion (as shown at left) during time-outs along with the cheerleaders to keep the fans stirred up. The 1998–99 roundballers went 23-11 on the season including a second-round showing in the NCAA Tournament. The Hogwild Band was also on hand as the LadyBacks won the NIT Tournament Championship game in Bud Walton.

In the fall of 1999, 280 students gathered on the rehearsal parking lot next to the U of A Tennis and Track Complex to form the newest edition of the Marching Razorback Band. Leading the group on the field were drum majors Chris Cansler, Shawn O'Kelley, and Brian Wolfe with Kendra Wilson as featured twirler. The photo at left captures the Razorback Band as they entered the field through the stadium chute prior to the University of Louisiana-Monroe game in Little Rock's War Memorial Stadium.

During the 1999–2000 marching season, the Arkansas Band performed halftime shows capitalizing on the jump and swing music popular that year, celebrating the centennial of Duke Ellington's birth and rocking to the sounds of the stalwart group Chicago.

At the half of the Middle Tennessee State game in October of 1999, the Razorback and MTS Bands joined in a combined show marching to the music of "Zoot Suit Riot," "Hey Pachuco," and "Jump, Jive, and Wail." As shown in the photo above, the two bands presented a 550-member strong performance to the crowd in Razorback Stadium.

When the regular football season ended in 1999, Arkansas had a 7-4 record, which was good enough to garner a bid to the Cotton Bowl game on January 1, 2000. The left photo shows the band in their final regular-season performance at the Mississippi State game played in Little Rock on November 20.

After a three-year hiatus, the Razorback Band reinstated their popular Band Spectacular in the Walton Arts Center in November 1999. Proceeds from the concert went toward funding the band's instrument and equipment needs.

The 2000 Cotton Bowl resurrected the old Razorback-Longhorn rivalry of the former SWC. And as before, both bands were present to give the teams the best support possible. The photos on this page document the Marching Razorbacks' presence in both the Cotton Bowl Parade and halftime presentation. With great gusto the Hogs won 27–6.

The Razorback basketball team went into a slump during the 1999–2000 season but managed to pull off a feat it had not managed since joining the SEC. Over four consecutive nights they finally won the SEC Tournament, earning one more invitation to the NCAA Big Dance. Their final season record was 19-15.

Early in the 1999–2000 school year, Athletic Director Frank Broyles announced plans to expand Razorback Stadium in Fayetteville to accommodate seventy thousand fans to the tune of many millions of dollars. And later he expressed his desire to move all the Little Rock games to Fayetteville. An uproar ensued, dividing the state along many different lines and resulting in a compromise that satisfied few. The plan called for three football games to be played in Little Rock for three of the following fifteen seasons, and for two games to be played in War Memorial Stadium the remaining years.

A highlight of the spring semester of 2000 is also considered one of the highlights of the Razorback Band's entire 130-year history. On Sunday, April 9, the U of A Wind Symphony presented a concert in Carnegie Hall in New York City as part of the Distinguished Ensemble Debut Series. The left photo was taken during that occasion.

Timothy Gunter

Timothy Gunter took over as the director of the Marching Razorbacks for the fall of 2000 and guided the record 318-member organization through one of its hottest pre-season "early week" rehearsals ever. The temperature in Arkansas rose so high on the first game day on September 2 in Little Rock (105 degrees) that the kick-off was postponed from 6 PM (99 degrees) to 8 PM (91 degrees). Gunter also allowed the band to wear their rehearsal T-shirts and shorts during the game (shown above) instead of their heavier uniforms.

Martin Reynolds

Gunter's assistant director for 2000–2001 was Martin Reynolds, and together the men mentored the Marching Razorbacks through their halftime performances in Fayetteville as Razorback Stadium underwent its multi-million dollar expansion. As can be seen below , the 30-by-107-feet SmartVision screen was working in the midst of the construction. Notice the band displayed on the screen.

For 2000–2001 the Marching Razorbacks presented their first half-time shows set to big band versions of "Birdland," "Elk's Parade," and "Big Noise from Winnetka." The second round of shows featured hits of Santana including "Black Magic Woman," "Evil Ways," and "Europa." And for their last shows the performers spotlighted the music of Harry Connick Jr.

Above, the 2000 Razorback majorettes and flag line enter Razorback Stadium ready to go into the pre-game ceremonies. Drum majors that season were Shawn O'Kelley, Brian Wolfe, and Chad Peevy.

At the Little Rock–played LSU game in November 2000, it rained, but that did not stop the Razorback Band from taking the field and spelling out the "Big A" for the team to run through.

With a 6-5 record in 2000 (3-3 in the SEC), the Hogs went to the Las Vegas Bowl on December 21 with 170 of the 313 member Razorback Band along for musical and school spirit support. UNLV won in their own back yard, 31–14.

As for the 2000–2001 basketball season, the Hogs went 20-11 finishing with a first round loss in the NCAA Tournament.

In the fall of 2000, Psi Chapter of Tau Beta Sigma celebrated its fiftieth anniversary on the U of A campus with a reunion of past and present members at the Clarion Hotel in Fayetteville.

The Wind Symphony poses above after a 2001 concert in Baum Walker Hall in the Walton Arts Center.

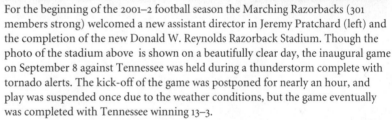

For the beginning of the 2001–2 football season the Marching Razorbacks (301 members strong) welcomed a new assistant director in Jeremy Pratchard (left) and the completion of the new Donald W. Reynolds Razorback Stadium. Though the photo of the stadium above is shown on a beautifully clear day, the inaugural game on September 8 against Tennessee was held during a thunderstorm complete with tornado alerts. The kick-off of the game was postponed for nearly an hour, and play was suspended once due to the weather conditions, but the game eventually was completed with Tennessee winning 13–3.

Though the whole world was shaken by the events of September 11, 2001, with the terrorist attacks on the World Trade Center in New York City, the Razorback Pep Band (shown right) joined the rest of humanity in trying to get back to normal by traveling to Tuscaloosa in support of the Hogs in their game against Alabama on September 22. The Crimson Tide won the tilt 31–10. Typically two busloads of band students made up the Pep Band as opposed to the required seven buses that usually carried the entire band to Little Rock games.

For the band's first halftime show following 9/11, the Marching Razorbacks presented a patriotic salute culminating in the left formation on the field during the game with Weber State in Fayetteville. The Hogs won the non-conference meeting 42–19. Later shows featured the music of Chuck Mangione and the rock group the Eagles.

Right, the Razorback Band musically cheered-on the Hogs from the stands as the team beat the seventeenth ranked Auburn Tigers 42–17 in Reynolds Razorback Stadium. The following week the Pep Band witnessed history when they watched the Razorbacks defeat the Ole Miss Tigers at Oxford in a record-breaking seven-overtime win of 58–56.

The majorette line for the Marching Razorbacks in 2001 included the women at right with Kendra Wilson (fifth from left) serving as featured twirler. Renessa Dunlap (center), herself a former featured twirler with the band, served as majorette coordinator for the group from 1997 to 2002. Drum majors for the season were Brian Wolfe, Mark Burnett, and Jennifer Pendergrass.

The Razorback football team finished the regular season with a 6-5 record with which they backed into another bid to play in the Cotton Bowl on New Year's Day 2002 against the powerhouse Oklahoma Sooners. The Razorback Band in the left photo closed out their marching season at home against Mississippi State with the Hogs winning 24–21.

Prior to the 2002 Cotton Bowl game played in Dallas, the Marching Razorback saxophone section posed for the above photo just before marching into the stadium with the rest of the band.

At the half of the 2002 Cotton Bowl the Razorback Band encored their popular "Eagles Show" from earlier in the season. Though the Hogs put up a valiant fight on the field, the tenth ranked Oklahoma Sooners won in the end 10–3.

The J. William Fulbright College of Arts and Sciences
presents the
75th Anniversary Celebration of the U of A Concert Bands

CONCERT BAND

Jeremy Pratchard, Conductor

WIND SYMPHONY

W. Dale Warren, Conductor

with Special Guests:
Donald Grantham, Lynn Klock, Wiff Rudd,
Richard "Doc" Worthington, & Eldon A. Janzen

Tuesday, February 26, 2002
7:30 pm
Walton Arts Center
Baum Walker Concert Hall
Fayetteville, Arkansas

Presented as part of the
Joy Pratt Markham Series

Among the concerts presented during the 2001–2 school year was one performed on February 26, 2002, commemorating the seventy-fifth anniversary season of the University of Arkansas Concert Band, the first such musical program having been given in the spring of 1927. A joint concert of the Wind Symphony and Concert Band in Baum Walker Hall honored the event with a premiere performance of the specially commissioned number "Fayetteville Bop" by Donald Grantham. Also performed was "Le Carnaval De Venise" featuring trumpet artist, Wiff Rudd of the U of A Music Department.

Although Nolan Richardson passed his five hundredth career collegiate win during the 2001–2 Razorback Basketball season, the Hogs managed only a 13-14 record under his tutelage that year. Prior to the team's final game of the season against Vanderbilt, the university bought out his contract and let him go in a highly publicized and extremely controversial set of circumstances. Assistant coach Mike Anderson led the team through the final game and into the SEC Tournament. Later in the spring, Stan Heath, fresh from coaching Kent State to the Elite Eight of the 2002 NCAA Tournament, was hired as the new basketball coach for the Hogs.

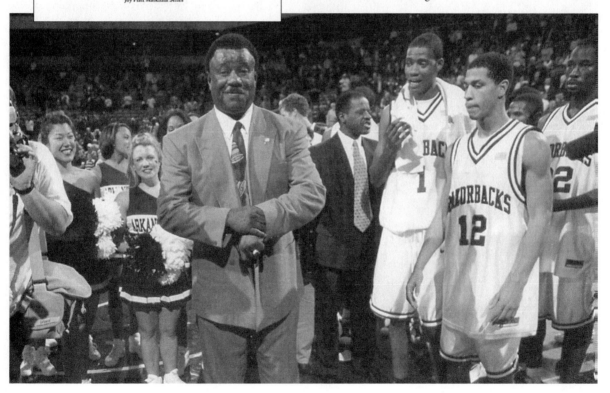

For the 2002–3 marching season of the Razorback Band the drum majors were Parker Denson, Stephanie Wilson, and Mark Burnett shown at left. With 285 members on the roster, the entire marching unit performed at all the in-state home games while a smaller uniformed Pep Band traveled to the regularly scheduled away games to support the gridiron Hogs.

Themed halftime shows for the Marching Razorbacks for 2002 included field performances of selections from *The Wizard of Oz* and *The Wiz*, a trio of 1970s hits representing a "Salute to Eight Track Tapes," and a tribute to the sounds of Motown. In addition, at Homecoming the band dedicated its halftime show to the men and women of the U. S. armed forces with songs representing each of the military branches.

Also, the Marching Razorbacks were guest performers at a high-school marching competition held in the fall of 2002 at Alma High School where a few of the brass members posed for the right photo.

The above photo shot from the upper deck of the south end zone showcases the large "A" formation the band created for the introduction of the Arkansas football players during pre-game festivities. Note the augmentation of the excitement on the field with the large screen display of various images on the turf and in the stands.

For at least three of the in-state home games in 2002, rain fell on the Saturday Hog football events resulting in the band being outfitted in inclement weather attire. The above photo shows the Marching Razorbacks in Little Rock's War Memorial Stadium in pre-game block band formation at the Troy State game.

Here is the ever-popular band secretary Connie Vick (center in tux) with jubilant band members after the annual Band Spectacular held in Walton Arts Center in mid-November 2002. Vick was one of the guest conductors during the concert.

Marching Razorback brass players, being the hams that they are, struck the above pose outside the travel buses prior to the exciting game with LSU in Little Rock. The Hogs upset the Tigers on November 29, 2002, sending Arkansas into the SEC title game with Georgia in the Georgia Dome the following week.

During halftime of the LSU game, the Razorback Band marched their popular "Salute to Eight Track Tapes" show before the partisan Arkansas crowd. With the win over the Tigers 21–20, the Hogs ended their regularly scheduled season with an 8-4 record.

This sideline view of the Marching Razorback Band during the pre-game show of the Georgia-Arkansas playoff game in the Georgia Dome on December 2, 2002, reflects the optimism that the band members had in the team in going for the conference championship. Unfortunately the Hogs lost to the Dogs 30–3, but they did muster a fifth bowl-game bid in as many years to play Minnesota in the Music City Bowl on December 30 in Nashville, Tennessee. Though the latter was a fun trip for the band, the team lost to the Golden Gophers 29–14.

With Stan Heath in his first year as head coach of the Razorback basketball team, the Hogwild Band showed its support during all the home games in 2002–3. Though the team had a losing season (9-19), the players at times displayed bursts of excellence and much promise for future seasons.

The Razorback Band entered the 2003 marching season with 298 members in its ranks and performed four different halftime shows for the two Little Rock and five Fayetteville home games. The photo at right shows the band entering the Reynolds Razorback Stadium for pre-game activities prior to the Tulsa game in September.

After a convincing win over the Texas Longhorns in Austin (38–28), the 2003 Hogs traveled to Little Rock for the season's third consecutive victory over North Texas. The Razorback Band's halftime shows for both the Tulsa and North Texas games featured drills set to four songs from *West Side Story*: "Maria," "One Hand, One Heart," "Mambo," and "Somewhere."

Following a successful September, the Razorbacks suffered a winless October, losing all three games that month to Auburn, Florida, and Ole Miss. At the Homecoming game against Auburn, the Razorback Band saluted Frank Broyles and his wife Barbara for their five decades of support of Arkansas athletics with a show highlighting the coach's favorite music—Glenn Miller's "In the Mood" and "Pennsylvania 6-5000." Note the empty seats in the lower east stands to the right in the above picture—that is the band's usual vantage point from which to cheer on the team.

For the Florida game in Fayetteville, the Razorback Band presented a halftime show centered around "Music of the Caribbean." Decked out in colorful tropical shirts, the band performed music with the U of A Steel Drum Band, Steel Pandemonium, which included "St. Thomas," "Marianne," and Harry Belafonte's "Jump in the Line."

Razorback trumpet players exhibit smiles all around prior to a game to be played in Reynolds Razorback Stadium in Fayetteville. For away games in 2003, members of the band formed a smaller Pep Band that traveled to the Texas, Alabama, Ole Miss, Kentucky, and LSU games in support of the U of A football team.

Head drum major for 2003 Stephanie Wilson is shown above on a ladder in front of the band leading one of the many "Woo Pig Sooie" cheers that typically are called during any Razorback football game.

Timothy Gunter (second from left), director of the Razorback Marching Band, had a very supportive staff that helped to create, rehearse, and fine-tune the band's performances on the field in 2003. They were (left to right) assistant director Jeremy Pratchard; graduate assistants Michael Parker and Jeremy Doss; percussion coordinator Aaron Ragsdale; front ensemble instructor Ashley Ragsdale; and flag corps coordinator Chris Kichline. Not pictured were band secretary Connie Vick and twirling coordinator Kendra Wilson. The voice of the Razorback Band was again Larry Shank.

A vital part of any marching band is its percussion section. And at the U of A, that is especially the case. Coordinated by Razorback Band alumnus Aaron Ragsdale in 2003, the section displayed a variety of percussion styles ranging from the swing of Glenn Miller to the sounds of the Caribbean, and from Broadway's *West Side Story* to the flourishes of Aaron Copland's exquisite melodies.

The fourth halftime show marched by the Razorback Band in 2003 was a tribute to Aaron Copland, widely regarded as the dean of American twentieth-century composers. This show was marched at the South Carolina game played in Little Rock, the New Mexico and Mississippi State games played in Fayetteville, and the Independence Bowl game against Missouri in Shreveport on December 31. Music included drills marched to "Rodeo," "Fanfare for the Common Man," and, as illustrated in the above photo, "Simple Gifts."

In 2003 the Razorback football team finished its season with a 9–4 season overall, a 4-4 SEC record, and a win in the Independence Bowl over Missouri 27–14. And the Razorback Band was on hand at all the games in full force or with the Pep Band to support the team in its efforts.

Concurrent with the marching season, the concert band season continued in 2003–4 with many students playing in both venues. The Wind Symphony is shown above in a fall concert directed by W. Dale Warren. Also on the year's calendar were presentations by the Symphonic Band, the Concert Band, and various smaller ensembles.

As in previous years, the Hogwild Band, the Lady Hogwild Basketball, and Volleyball Bands performed in Bud Walton Arena and Barnhill Arena during 2003–4 to spur on the athletes to victory.

A FINAL WORD FROM THE AUTHOR

The reader can see from what has been written in these pages that the band program at the University of Arkansas at Fayetteville has undergone a tremendous journey. From its beginnings as a small ragtag group of cadets supporting the cadet corps in drill maneuvers on the lawn in front of University Hall in the 1870s to the magnificent Razorback marching, Hogwild-playing, concert-serenading organization it is today, it has always been an axis around which musical excitement has been generated on campus.

And it has been a family affair all along. The Razorback Band family. As with all families, it has had its ups and downs, triumphs and defeats, accomplishments and disappointments, pride and despair. But it has always been a group of individuals dedicated to the goal of presenting the University of Arkansas in the best possible light.

Unfortunately as with all families, we eventually lose those who preceded us. But they are always a part of our legacy as members of the Razorback Band family who provided us with a rich heritage to cherish and hopefully to cause us to be ever proud to have followed them.

Those who are currently performing in the various arms of the Razorback band program in the here and now are shouldering and experiencing the responsibilities and pleasures of the band, adding to the reputation of an already renowned and legendary group of brothers and sisters. And they are making memories today that will be treasured and remembered for years to come.

The hope to look forward to is that there will be others who will add to the ranks in the future to continue the tradition that has provided so many with the spirit and excitement that has made the Razorback Band such a vibrant part of the alma mater of which we are all proud to call our own—the University of Arkansas.

1874–91	Presumed to be student directors only
1892–94	Frank Barr, student leader
1896?–17	Frank Barr, director
1917–20	Ben H. Winkleman, student director
1920–26	Owen C. Mitchell
1926–27	Patrick F. Freyer
1927–November 1940	Francis Judah Foutz
November 1940–February 1941	Gene Witherspoon, student director
February 1941–August 1943	Robert W. Winslow
August 1943–June 1944	Merton S. Zahrt, interim director
June 1944–September 1945	Dr. Robert W. Winslow
September 1945–January 1946	R. W. Willis, interim director
February 1946–May 1948	Dr. Merton S. Zahrt
1948–55	Edmund J. (E. J.) Marty
1955–56	Roger Widder
1956–70	Dr. Richard R. ("Doc") Worthington
1970–80, 1982–85	Eldon Janzen
1981, 1985–87	Chalon Ragsdale
1987–91	Jim Robken
1991–2000	W. Dale Warren
2000–	Timothy W. Gunter

APPENDIX 1

BAND DIRECTORS OF THE UNIVERSITY OF ARKANSAS-FAYETTEVILLE MARCHING BAND

1885	C. A. Davies	1918	Ben Winkleman	
1886	R. L. Rutherford	1919	Ben Winkleman	
1890	A. J. Newman	1920		
1892	J. E. Kirkham	1921		
1893	R. H. Williams	1922	R. Harris	
1894	C. D. Head	1923		
1895	C. G. Price	1924	Tommy Warner	
1896	H. D. Mann	1925	Welton Renner	
1897	H. D. Mann	1926	James A. Carruth	
1898	George W. Shuler E. D. Kidder	1927	James A. Carruth	
		1928	John E. Stair	
1899	C. W. Hannah E. D. Kidder	1929	Fred Raedels	
		1930	Norman Warnock	
1900	E. L. L. Keeler	1931	Norman Warnock	
1901	C. M. Conway	1932	Norman Warnock	
1902	W. D. Dickinson	1933	Norman Warnock	
1903	F. A. Garrett	1934	Norman Warnock Harry Crumpler	
1904	Charles G. Lueker			
1905	Charles G. Lueker	1935	Harry Crumpler	
1906	Charles G. Lueker	1936	Harry Crumpler Judge Chapman	
1907	Charles G. Lueker			
1908		1937	Judge Chapman	
1909	W. T. Dorough	1938	Judge Chapman	
1910		1939	Jimmy Baker Raymond Jackson Jack Joyce	
1911				
1912				
1913		1940		
1914		1941	A. F. Thomas	
1915	E. L. Woofin	1942	A. F. Thomas	
1916	Scott Johnson	1943	Dale Bumpers	
1917	Ben Winkleman	1944		
		1945	J. P. Crumpler	

DRUM MAJORS OF THE UNIVERSITY OF ARKANSAS-FAYETTEVILLE MARCHING RAZORBACK BAND

1946	J. P. Crumpler	1969	Gary Ricketts Tommy Thompson
1947	J. P. Crumpler	1970	Tommy Thompson Dwight Estes
1948	Jeannine Hartley		
1949	Jeannine Hartley	1971	Dwight Estes Sanford Tollette
1950	Jeannine Hartley		
1951	Tommy Gray	1972	Sanford Tollette Bill Irwin
1952	Tommy Gray		
1953	Bob Griffin	1973	Ken McIntosh
1954	Bob Griffin	1974	Ken McIntosh Grady Core
1955	Bob Griffin		
1956	Richard Carroll	1975	Grady Core Joel Clark
1957	Gerald Reed Paul Lloyd Martin	1976	Grady Core Joel Clark
1958	George Jernigan Clyde Pope	1977	Joel Clark Tony Logue
1959	Richard Bush	1978	Tony Logue Jon Beard
1960	Richard Bush		
1961	Jim Bob Norwood Richard Burton	1979	Tony Logue Alex Dunlap
1962	Jim Bob Norwood Sandy Porter	1980	Alex Dunlap Carl Mouton
1963	Sandy Porter Bill Woolly	1981	Alex Dunlap Carl Mouton
1964	Sandy Porter Bill Woolly	1982	Steve Palen Russell Morris
1965	Sandy Porter Bill Woolly	1983	Steve Palen Russell Morris
1966	Bill Woolly John Richardson	1984	Russell Morris Paul Simkins
1967	John Richardson Gary Ricketts	1985	Paul Simkins Sandy Stephenson
1968	John Richardson Gary Ricketts	1986	Tom Nelson Mike Ferguson

1987	Mike Ferguson Kevin Miller	1997	Shane Jennings Rocky Long Shawn O'Kelley
1988	Kevin Miller Marsha Wilson	1998	Shane Jennings Rocky Long Shawn O'Kelley
1989	Caryn Hobson Shane Jones	1999	Chris Cansler Shawn O'Kelley Brian Wolfe
1990	Shane Jones Scott Howard	2000	Shawn O'Kelley Brian Wolfe Chad Peevy
1991	Scott Howard Matt Pratt	2001	Brian Wolfe Mark Burnett Jennifer Pendergrass
1992	Scott Howard Matt Pratt	2002	Parker Denson Mark Burnett Stephanie Wilson
1993	Matt Pratt Chris Cansler	2003	Stephanie Wilson Charles Frazier Jennifer Pendergrass
1994	Matt Pratt Chris Cansler Doug Blevins		
1995	Chris Cansler Shane Jennings Tonya Blevins Landon Shockey		
1996	Chris Cansler Shane Jennings Rocky Long		